WALLS

BY JAMES CROSS GIBLIN

LITTLE, BROWN AND COMPANY
BOSTON   TORONTO

·1984·

W·A·L·L·S

DEFENSES THROUGHOUT HISTORY

FIRST EDITION

Library of Congress Cataloging in Publication Data

Giblin, James.
    Walls : defenses throughout history.

    Summary: Discusses why and how walls have been
constructed throughout history, around cities, castles,
even countries.
    1. Walls — Juvenile literature. 2. Fortification —
Juvenile literature. 3. Attack and defense (Military
science) — Juvenile literature. [1. Walls — History.
2. Fortification — History] I. Title.
UG407.G5 1984   623'.12   84-15444
ISBN 0-316-30954-0

MP

Published simultaneously in Canada
by Little, Brown & Company (Canada) Limited

PRINTED IN THE UNITED STATES OF AMERICA

For Elizabeth Isele

ACKNOWLEDGMENTS

≡III≡II≡II≡II≡II≡II≡II≡II≡II≡II≡II≡II≡II≡II≡II≡II≡II≡II≡II≡II≡II≡II≡II≡II≡III

For their help in providing research material, illustrations, advice, and support, the author thanks the following institutions and individuals: The American Museum of Natural History, New York; Lawrence and Natalie Bober; The British Museum, London; The British Tourist Authority; The Cleveland Museum of Art; Fort Ticonderoga Museum; French Embassy, Press and Information Division; French Government Tourist Office; German Information Center, New York; Hoover Institution on War, Revolution and Peace, Stanford; Hsinhua News Agency; Imperial War Museum, London; Japan National Tourist Organization; The Library of Congress, Washington; Murray Liebman; The Metropolitan Museum of Art, New York; Morley Library, Painesville, Ohio; Jim Murphy; Musée Memorial de Verdun, France; The National Archives, Washington; National Park Service, U.S. Department of the Interior; The New York Public Library; Beatrice Schenk de Regniers; Royal Commission on Historical Monuments (England); Southend Air Photography, Ltd., London; The U.S. Air Force; The Welsh Office, Cardiff, Wales.

"War is as old as humanity, and the construction of fortresses as old as war. The first buildings erected by man seem, indeed, to have been protecting walls."

from *Medieval Cities* (1925)
by the Belgian historian
Henri Pirenne

CONTENTS

WALLS

A WALL MADE OF
MAMMOTH BONES

An Ice Age camp, surrounded by a wall of mammoth bones
(American Museum of Natural History)

It is early in the morning of a cold, cloudy day in central Europe more than twenty-five thousand years ago. A band of Ice Age hunters clad in furs and armed with flint knives has just left their camp. They are on their way to track a herd of woolly mammoths that scouts have seen passing through the valley below.

From excavations of many campsites, we know that mammoths were extremely important to these Ice Age people, who lived at a time when glaciers covered much of the earth. During the long, harsh winters when nothing could grow, the people depended on mammoth meat for food. They made clothing and blankets from the animals' thick, dark fur, and tent coverings from their hides. Out of mammoth bones they carved spearpoints, tools, and even small figures of animals and people.

Woolly mammoths were large, elephantlike creatures. The skeleton of one found in the Siberian region of the Soviet Union measured over sixteen feet from its forehead to its tail. It stood nine feet, four inches tall, and had curving tusks nine-and-a-half feet long. Because Ice Age trees were often no bigger than bushes, people used mammoth tusks instead of wooden poles to prop up their shelters. Sometimes they weighted the skin coverings of the shelters with mammoth skulls to keep them from flapping in the breeze.

Ice Age people also gathered mammoth leg bones, backbones, tusks, and rib bones, and piled them in huge defensive walls around their camps. The ruins of such camps, with their walls, have been found buried deep underground in what is today Czechoslovakia and the western Soviet Union. Scientists estimate that each camp probably housed between thirty and a hundred people.

It must have taken a great deal of effort to build the protective walls. First the bones had to be removed from mammoths that were killed in the hunt, or from animals that were found where they had died naturally. Then the bones had to be transported back to the camp. Everyone who lived in the camp, young and old, must have been enlisted in the task, for mammoth bones were by no means light. A dried mammoth skull complete with tusks could weigh as much as 220 pounds. And other mammoth bones were almost as heavy.

No one knows exactly why Ice Age people built these walls of mammoth bones. Perhaps they were intended to protect the people from raids by wolves and other predatory animals. Perhaps they were used to defend the camp if human enemies tried to attack it. Or perhaps they simply provided an additional barrier against the icy winter winds that swept across the central European plain.

*   *   *

Ever since the Ice Age, people in all parts of the world have built walls to protect themselves. Such walls have guarded cities, castles, and sometimes entire countries. They have been constructed of logs, stones, bricks, concrete, or simply mounds of hardened earth. They have been dozens of feet high and as much as fifty feet thick. Several of them have stretched out across the land for hundreds or even thousands of miles. When these walls were designed to keep out enemy armies, they were called *fortifications*.

This book highlights, in words and pictures, some of the most unusual and impressive walls that people have built throughout history to defend themselves. It tells why and how the walls were constructed, and describes the dramatic events that took place on and around them. It also shows how defensive walls have had to change in the face of ever more powerful attack weapons.

Many of the walls included here, like Hadrian's Wall and the Great Wall of China, are still standing and are visited by thousands of tourists every year. But the remains of others can only be found buried deep under the earth's surface. Such is the case with the legendary walls of Jericho, located in what is today West Jordan.

OPPOSITE: *The walls of Harlech Castle in Wales* (The British Tourist Authority)

ANCIENT WALLED CITIES

Tower and walls of Jericho at night (American Museum of
Natural History)

A full moon shone down on the city of Jericho on a summer night in 6500 B.C., almost eighty-five hundred years ago. The thousand or so inhabitants slept soundly, confident that the massive stone wall around the city would protect them from any surprise attack by their enemies.

Soldiers stood guard atop the wall, which was twenty-one feet high, and faced with plaster. In front of it stretched a water-filled ditch, fifteen feet wide and nine feet deep, that had been cut out of solid rock. Other guards peered out at the surrounding countryside through slits in a forty-foot-high stone tower that rose behind the wall and was connected to it.

Situated in a desert oasis north of the Dead Sea, Jericho was probably the first city in the world. Evidence of human settlement dating back to 8000 B.C. has been found there, along with the remains of a wall built as early as 7000 B.C. The wall encompassed an area of more than ten acres, and was intended to keep out the marauding nomadic tribes that often threatened the settlement.

No part of Jericho's wall or guard tower remains standing today. But archaeologists have dug up the stone foundations of both, and from them they can estimate how thick and tall the structures were. The foundations also reveal that the walls of Jericho were destroyed and rebuilt many times over the centuries. The most famous attack on them occurred during the Hebrew leader Joshua's campaign to reclaim the promised land of Israel for his people. The Canaanites occupied Jericho at the time.

As recorded in the Old Testament, the story says that the Lord told Joshua to march around the city wall with his soldiers once a day for six days. Seven priests were to follow behind the soldiers and blow loudly on seven trumpets made from rams' horns, as they paraded. Everyone else on the march would remain silent.

On the seventh day, the story continues, Joshua and his people were to march around Jericho seven times. Then, after the seventh circuit was completed, everyone would stand in place and look toward the city walls. The priests would blow a single, long blast on their trumpets, all the people would give a great shout, and, the Lord said, "the wall of the city shall fall down flat."

Joshua followed the Lord's instructions carefully and on the seventh day, when everyone shouted, the walls of Jericho did come tumbling down. Joshua and his people rushed forward, climbed over the fallen stones, and seized the city.

That's how the Bible says it happened, but it's unlikely that a shout could have brought down thick walls made of stone and mortar. Some Israeli archaeologists today believe that Joshua broke through the walls in a different way. They call his tactics an early example of psychological warfare.

OPPOSITE: *Excavated foundation of guard tower at Jericho* (L. H. Bober)

When the defenders of Jericho saw Joshua's people marching around the walls on the first day, they were probably puzzled, and reacted by reaching for their weapons. But after Joshua had repeated the march five more times in as many days without making any move against the city, the defenders probably relaxed their guard. Thus they were unprepared when, on the seventh day, the Hebrews broke the pattern, gave a great shout, and stormed the walls of the city. On that morning, the gates of the city may not even have been barred.

By whatever means the walls of Jericho did fall, there is firm archaeological evidence that the city was destroyed sometime between 1400 and 1250 B.C. According to the Bible, that would have been in the time of Joshua.

The peoples of many other ancient cultures and civilizations followed the example set by the residents of Jericho and surrounded their cities with defensive walls. In fact, in the Chinese language the character for "wall" is the same as the one for "city," and from the time the Chinese began to settle in cities around 2000 B.C., all of their cities were walled.

Historical records tell us that ancient peoples all over the world chose a place to build a city with great care. The spot had to have a year-round supply of fresh water. Around it there had to be a fertile countryside that could provide food for the city's population. People also tried to find a site that could be defended easily against attacks by envious neighbors or nomadic tribes. Natural defenses such as hilltops, mountain plateaus, or peninsulas — projections of land surrounded on three sides by water — were utilized whenever possible.

When cities were built on plains, where there were no natural defenses, huge man-made walls became an absolute necessity for the safety of the inhabitants. One such place was Mesopotamia, modern-day Iraq. There some of the greatest cities in the ancient world sprang up around 2500 B.C. — more than four thousand years ago — on the flat plains that stretch between the Tigris and Euphrates rivers.

Because stone and wood were scarce, the walls of most Mesopotamian cities were made of baked mud brick. From written records and archaeological excavations, we know that Uruk, the largest city in southern Mesopotamia, was surrounded by two mud-brick walls, the outer of which had a circumference of over seven miles. The inner wall was more than sixteen feet thick. The outer surfaces of the walls were covered with plaster and sometimes they were painted with colorful decorations.

The walls of Uruk have long since crumbled, but we can read a description of them in the Mesopotamian poem *Gilgamesh:* "The outer wall shines with the brilliance of copper, the inner wall has no equal. . . . Climb upon the wall of Uruk; walk along it, I say. Regard the foundation and examine the building; is it not burnt brick and good?"

The walls of other cities in Mesopotamia were even more impressive. Those around Ur, which is identified in the Old Testament as the home of Abraham, father of the Hebrew people, were reported to be over forty feet thick. The walls of ancient Babylon, another Mesopotamian city, rose to a height of more than eighty feet. To reinforce Babylon's wall, towers were erected all along it at intervals of 140 feet, and a deep moat was dug in front of it.

One of the major duties of a Mesopotamian king was to keep the walls of his city in good repair, and to destroy the walls of enemy cities he and his army conquered. It's well to remember that everything was on a smaller scale in ancient times. A large city in Mesopotamia might have had a population of five to ten thousand people, and an attacking army would probably have had no more than a few hundred soldiers, a thousand at most.

Mesopotamian armies used many different methods and weapons to break through an enemy city's walls. If there was a moat in front of the wall, the attackers, under cover of darkness, would try to bridge it with planking. Then soldiers would cross the planking and chip at weak places in the wall with tools like crowbars, hoping to make a hole.

A more effective method that was often employed was *mining*. Teams of attacking soldiers would attempt to dig a tunnel under the wall. As they moved forward they braced the tunnel with wooden timbers. Sometimes, instead of going all the way through, they stopped when they were directly under the wall, erected their timbers, covered them with grease, and set fire to them. As soon as the wood began to burn, the soldiers hurried out of the tunnel. If everything went according to plan, the tunnel would fall in when the timbers burned through, and a section of the wall would collapse with it. Then the attacking soldiers could rush through the opening into the city.

While soldiers tunneled under the wall, giant *battering rams* might be assaulting it above ground. These rams were usually made from the trunks of thick, tall trees. The trunks were shod with iron at one end, and set in a strong wooden framework mounted on wheels. Often two rams were attached to a single frame, side by side, in order to double the weapon's destructive force.

Squads of soldiers shoved the rams against the city wall over and over again. The rams' wooden framework helped to protect the soldiers from

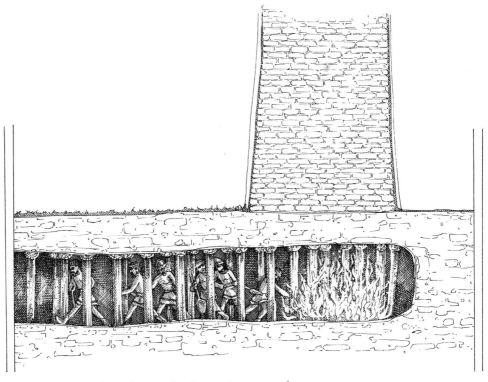

Soldiers setting fire to the wooden braces in a tunnel

arrows shot by defenders standing atop the wall. Additional protection came from wet animal hides that covered the frames so that flaming arrows would not set them ablaze.

To keep a ram from working, the defenders of the city tried to catch its head in the loop of a chain that they dropped from the wall. The attackers, in turn, attempted to remove the chain with long-handled hooks so that the ram would once more be free to batter the wall.

Another huge attack weapon was the *siege tower*, which was used by Assyrian armies in Mesopotamia as early as 1000 B.C. Siege towers were wheeled wooden structures, two or more stories high. They had several platforms on which archers could stand, and, like battering rams, they were usually covered with damp animal skins in order to repel attack by fire.

Foot soldiers moved the siege towers about like wooden tanks while the archers fired their arrows at the defenders on the city's wall. Eventually the soldiers pushed the towers right up to the wall itself. Then the archers and other fighters on the topmost platforms could leap onto the top of the wall and engage the defenders in hand-to-hand combat.

Stone relief of Assyrians storming a city (The Metropolitan Museum of Art, Purchase, 1955, Joseph Pulitzer Bequest)

Relief of Assyrian army besieging a city in Mesopotamia (The British Museum)

Siege towers and battering rams helped the Assyrians to destroy the walls of Babylon in 689 B.C. But King Nebuchadnezzar rebuilt them in even grander style less than a century later. He dug a deeper moat and increased the height of the outer wall to an incredible eighty-five feet, eight inches. Not content with that, the king ordered the construction of an entirely new moat and a second wall within the old wall. Now Babylon was protected by a double line of moats and mud-brick walls.

The walls of many ancient cities were destroyed and rebuilt many times over. Jerusalem, for instance, was walled by King David, who captured the city from the Jebusites around 1000 B.C., and the walls were strengthened by his son King Solomon. Solomon also built his historic temple in Jerusalem about 950 B.C.

In succeeding centuries Jerusalem was captured by the Egyptians, the Babylonians, the Persians, the Romans, the Muslims, and Christian Crusaders, all of whom battered the walls with various weapons, and then rebuilt them after they occupied the city. The Romans, in particular, extended and enlarged the original walls.

When the Muslims recaptured Jerusalem from the Crusaders in 1187, they restored the walls on the foundations of those the Romans had constructed centuries earlier. These are the walls that still surround the Old City of Jerusalem today.

The famous Western, or "Wailing," Wall was not part of the ancient fortifications around Jerusalem. It was one side of the enclosure that protected King Solomon's Temple. After the Babylonians destroyed the temple in 586 B.C., the people of Jerusalem gathered by the wall to bemoan the temple's fate. From then on it was called the Wailing Wall and became a sacred place to all Jews.

For a long time people believed that the remaining section of the Western Wall actually dated back to Solomon's day. But now most agree that it was erected by the Romans during the time of King Herod, ruler of Jerusalem when Jesus was born.

Scale model of Jerusalem and its walls in the time of King Herod
(L. H. Bober)

The Western Wall in Jerusalem today (L. H. Bober)

THE WALLED CITY
OF CARCASSONNE

The walls of Carcassonne (French Government Tourist Office)

The Roman Empire was at its height just before and after the birth of Christ. When Roman armies conquered a region in what is today Spain, France, or Germany, they usually built a fortified town from which they could maintain control over the area.

The Romans had a ritual that they always followed after the location for a new town had been chosen. First they marked off the outer limits of the town with stakes. Then they plowed a furrow all around the site. The plowed earth was thrown inward and symbolized the town's future wall. The furrow represented the deep ditch or moat that would be dug outside the wall. The plow was lifted and the earth left unfurrowed at those places where the gates of the town would stand.

One of the most famous walled cities the Romans laid out was Carcassonne, in southern France. It's easy to understand why the Romans decided to build a fortified settlement there. The site of the future city was on the right bank of the Aude River, atop a hill that could be defended from all sides. To prevent raids by local tribes, the Romans surrounded the settlement with a high wall of stone and brick, interrupted at intervals by square stone *watchtowers*.

According to legend, Carcassonne got its name much later, in the ninth century, when the emperor Charlemagne was besieging the city. The siege had gone on for five years and the city's supply of food was almost exhausted.

No one knew what to do until an old woman, Dame Carcas, thought of a plan. She roasted one of the last remaining pigs in the city, stuffed it with grain, and carried it to the top of the city wall. After tying a rope around it, she lowered the pig down over the wall, where Charlemagne's soldiers could clearly see it. To make sure they looked up, the city's warning bell was rung.

When the pig was halfway down, Dame Carcas shook the rope, and grain shot out of the animal's mouth. This convinced Charlemagne and his men that the city still had plenty of food, and they withdrew. The siege was lifted, and Dame Carcas was hailed as a hero.

In gratitude the inhabitants named the city Carcassonne. "Carcas" honored Dame Carcas, and "sonne" — which means "ring" in French — referred to the bell that rang as part of her plan. Today a statue of Dame Carcas stands in the old section of Carcassonne.

This legend makes a good story, but unfortunately it isn't true. The original Roman builders of the city called it Carcaso, and the French later lengthened that name to Carcassonne. As far as anyone knows, there was no Dame Carcas — and no pig stuffed with grain.

When the Roman Empire collapsed during the fifth century A.D., Carcassonne was seized by a Germanic tribe, the Visigoths. It was a time of

Dame Carcas lowering the pig

great unrest, with many rival tribes on the march, attacking and plundering as they went. To protect their new conquest from such raids, the Visigoths expanded and strengthened the walls around Carcassonne.

They replaced the square watchtowers of the Romans with towers that were rounded on the outside. Archers standing at openings in the round towers could see attackers approaching from any direction, and could aim their arrows more accurately.

The Visigoths left no openings in the lower halves of the towers because they believed that solid stone walls would better resist enemy battering rams. There were large openings, however, at the top of the towers on the sides facing the city, through which rocks and other weapons could be hoisted up to the defenders.

The towers rose a story higher than the wall and were linked to it with wooden drawbridges. If an enemy managed to gain control of a section of wall, the drawbridges leading to the nearest towers could be lifted or destroyed. When that happened the enemy soldiers could go no further, and were at the mercy of bowmen stationed on the top stories of the neighboring towers.

The walls and towers of Carcassonne did their job well. For almost three hundred years the Visigoths defended the city successfully against attacks by the Franks, Burgundians, and other tribes. It wasn't until the year 725 that a Muslim army from Spain besieged and finally captured Carcassonne.

French forces drove out the Muslims in 752, and from then on various groups fought for control of the city. By the twelfth century it was in French hands again. But bands of rebels against the ruling Catholic church, as well as armies from Spain, constantly threatened it. To fend off possible attacks by these enemies, the French repaired and strengthened the old city wall of the Visigoths.

The wall faced one of its greatest tests in September 1240, when a rebel leader laid siege to Carcassonne. After crossing the Aude River, the attacking forces occupied a district located just outside one of the main gates to the city. The defenders considered sending out a force to fight them, until they saw how many crossbowmen the enemy had. The crossbow was a deadly weapon with a tremendous range. A bolt shot from one might travel as far as 370 or 380 yards.

The attackers destroyed a monastery in the district they controlled and used the timber from it to build a *palisade,* or fence of stakes, to protect themselves. Then they set up a *mangonel,* a huge device that hurled heavy stones, and aimed it at the city wall. But the defenders were prepared. They hauled a rock-throwing machine of their own to the top of the wall and aimed it at the mangonel. Whenever a squad of enemy soldiers tried to fire

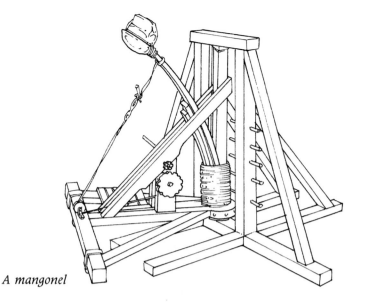

A mangonel

their weapon, the defenders showered them with a fresh hail of rocks. At last the enemy abandoned the mangonel and launched a different kind of attack.

Late at night they began to tunnel under one of the towers in the city wall, just as the Assyrians had tunneled under the city walls of their enemies hundreds of years before. The defenders heard them coming, though, and quickly built a stone wall within the ground floor of the tower to reinforce it. When the enemy set fire to the wooden supports in the tunnel, it caved in, and part of the front wall of the tower fell with it. But the second wall kept the rest of the tower from collapsing.

Despite this setback, the enemy wasn't about to give up. They dug six more tunnels at different places along the wall, and each time the defenders managed to block them in one way or another.

Once the attackers got into the city only to find themselves facing an inner wall of wooden stakes, manned by archers. Realizing that they would be mowed down if they tried to advance, the attackers beat a hasty retreat through their tunnel.

Another time the enemy soldiers were digging away beneath the wall when suddenly their crowbars and shovels broke through into empty space. They had entered a tunnel that the defenders of the city had dug to meet theirs. With shouts and cries the defenders raced into the enemy's tunnel and chased the startled soldiers back the way they had come. Then the defenders blocked the tunnel with a strong *paling,* a barrier of wooden pickets.

While all this tunneling was going on, the enemy continued to fire their crossbows at the defenders atop the walls. They also hurled rocks over the walls, and even the rotting bodies of dead animals, which they hoped would demoralize the defenders and spread disease.

The defenders' spirits remained high in spite of the constant assaults. They had plenty of meat and grain in their warehouses and were confident that help would come before the food supplies ran out.

At last, on a Sunday morning in early October, the enemy gathered all of its soldiers and crossbowmen for a frontal assault on the main gate of the city. The defenders met them with such a heavy rain of rocks, arrows, and boiling oil that they were forced to withdraw. A week later the enemy tried another mass attack, and again they were repulsed. This time a number of enemy soldiers were killed or wounded, but the defenders didn't lose a single man.

That proved to be the last enemy attack. On Monday, October 11, the attackers heard that a detachment of the French army was on its way to help the defenders of Carcassonne. The enemy leaders knew that they had no chance of succeeding now. That night, almost a month after the siege began, they ordered their men to withdraw. When the defenders looked out from the stone ramparts of Carcassonne the next morning, there were no enemy soldiers in sight.

The walls of Carcassonne had withstood the siege, but they were badly scarred. Since the city was an important outpost in southern France, King Louis IX ordered his engineers to strengthen and extend the ramparts. He wanted to make sure that no enemy dared to attack the city again.

A great *barbican,* or guard tower, large enough to house fifteen hundred soldiers, was built below the city on the banks of the Aude River. From the barbican a walled ramp led to a new outer city wall, studded with towers and turrets. Inside this outer wall was the old city wall of the Visigoths. All told the two walls around Carcassonne contained forty-eight towers and five heavily fortified gates.

King Louis's engineers included several *posterns,* or private gates, at protected places along the outer wall. These posterns were small openings, usually six feet high by three feet wide, and they were placed at least twenty feet above the ground so that they could be reached only by ladders. In case of a siege, messengers and spies descended from the posterns at night on rope ladders, and the city was able to maintain contact with the world outside.

After the engineers and builders finished their work, Carcassonne was one of the strongest and most beautiful walled cities in western Europe. Over the years that followed the city's walls proved their worth. They stopped Edward the Black Prince of England — called "black" because he wore black armor — when he attacked the city with a large force in 1355.

The road into the Old City of Carcassonne (French Government Tourist Office)

Only time and changing conditions weakened the walls of Carcassonne. As the central government of France became stronger, cities like Carcassonne were no longer threatened with attack by local lords and barons. And the city was no longer needed as a military outpost after France concluded a border treaty with Spain in 1659. Inspired by the peaceful mood, a large new city, Ville Basse, grew across the river. Meanwhile, people stopped repairing the old city walls, and eventually many sections crumbled and fell.

The walls were restored and rebuilt in the nineteenth century by Eugène Viollet-le-Duc, a French architect and writer who devoted his life to preserving France's architectural heritage. Today more than a thousand people still live and work along the narrow, winding streets of the old city. Thousands more visit Carcassonne each year to see for themselves what a walled city of the Middle Ages was like.

OPPOSITE: *The walls of Carcassonne from a distance* (French Embassy, Press and Information Division)
INSET: *Looking down from the Old City of Carcassonne* (French Government Tourist Office)

HADRIAN'S WALL

A section of Hadrian's Wall (The British Tourist Authority)

The Roman soldier shivers as he gazes out from the top of Hadrian's Wall at the rolling lands of northern England. It is a chilly October morning in 135 A.D., and a ground fog obscures the view.

The soldier leans against the protective five-foot-high *parapet* on the north side of the wall's flat top, and peers through the mist. Is that a band of roving barbarians out there? He looks more closely. No, it's just the shadow of a hill.

With a sigh of relief, the soldier turns away from the parapet and continues his patrol along the great stone wall. It rises fifteen feet above the surrounding countryside and stretches to a width of almost ten feet. If the soldier were to walk its entire length, he would cover a distance of more than seventy miles.

Hadrian's Wall is one of the best-known examples of a defensive wall meant to protect not just a town or city but an entire country. It bears the name of the Roman emperor Hadrian, who ordered its construction after he visited Rome's northernmost colony, England, in 122 A.D. The Roman army had subdued southern England, but wild tribes from the north were still raiding the border regions. Hadrian and his generals decided that a mighty wall was the only thing that would stop them.

Wanting the wall to be as efficient as possible, Hadrian's engineers chose to build it at the narrowest point in northern England. There the country is only a little more than seventy miles wide from coast to coast. It is a landscape of rolling moors and low hills, without the mountains that would have provided cover for hostile tribes and made building the wall more difficult.

Over ten thousand people took part in the construction of the wall. They included Roman soldiers, and men recruited from conquered English tribes. The laborers were organized into units of eighty and, judging by inscriptions found on the wall, they probably worked in leapfrog fashion. As a unit completed one section, it would move past the neighboring unit and start in on the next section assigned to it.

The stones used to face the wall on both sides were generally wedge-shaped. Their surfaces measured eight or nine inches by ten or eleven inches, and the wedges were as much as twenty inches long. These stones had to be transported from quarries seven or eight miles away. In hilly country, workers carried the stones on their backs; where the land was level enough, the stones were hauled in wagons.

The mortar used in the wall was much like today's concrete. It was made of lime mixed with sand, gravel, and water, and was very tough. The interior of the wall was filled with rubble — a mixture of small rocks and pebbles, held together with mortar like the facing stones.

Approximately every four miles along the wall, laborers built a large

Reconstructed Roman fort along Hadrian's Wall (The British Tourist Authority)

fort. These forts covered four or five acres and contained barracks for as many as a thousand soldiers or five hundred cavalrymen, with stables for their horses. Stone walls five to eight feet thick enclosed the forts, and the northern wall was usually part of Hadrian's Wall itself. The forts had four gates, one in each wall, and outside the southern gate there was often a village of wooden dwellings, where the wives and children of the soldiers lived.

Besides the forts, structures called *milecastles* stood at intervals of a little less than a mile all along the wall. Each milecastle measured about sixty feet by fifty feet and was manned by patrols of forty or fifty soldiers. The northern wall of the milecastle was part of the main wall and contained a large, well-defended gate. There was another gate in the southern wall.

Between each milecastle, at equal distances, rose two watchtowers. These towers were small, two-story stone structures that were built directly into the wall itself. Four soldiers were usually assigned to each tower. Two stood guard on the top story, watching the surrounding landscape through peepholes, while on the floor below, the other two rested, ate, or played dice.

If any point along the wall was attacked by a hostile tribe, signals were sent from watchtower to watchtower, from milecastle to milecastle. Soldiers from nearby towers and milecastles could race along the top of the wall to the aid of their neighbors. If additional help was needed, soldiers and cavalry from the nearest fort sped to the endangered sector by means of the broad stone road that ran directly south of the wall.

Some historians have said that lead pipes or speaking tubes were built into the wall between the watchtowers. Through these pipes soldiers could sound the alarm if they saw an enemy coming. It's a clever idea, but no evidence of such tubes has been found. Besides, they would hardly have been needed since the watchtowers were close enough for a trumpet blast to be heard from one to another.

The defenses of Hadrian's Wall didn't end with the forts, milecastles, and watchtowers. Leaving nothing to chance, the Roman builders also dug a V-shaped ditch, twenty-seven feet wide by nine feet deep, on the north side of the wall. Beyond the ditch they piled up the earth they had excavated and made a second wall.

And that wasn't all. To the south of the wall, on the other side of the stone road, the Romans dug an even deeper ditch and heaped the earth and rubble from it in huge mounds along both banks.

Many people have wondered why, if their enemies were to the north, the Romans felt it necessary to build such massive fortifications on the south

Remains of a Roman granary at Housesteads on Hadrian's Wall
(The British Tourist Authority)

OPPOSITE: *A couple walking along Hadrian's Wall* (The British Tourist Authority)

side, where supposedly friendly tribes lived. Perhaps it was because the Romans feared the southern tribes would join forces with their kinsmen if the tribes from the north succeeded in breaking through the wall. Or perhaps the Romans were simply following through on something one of their generals, Agricola, is reported to have said: "It has long been my opinion that the back of a general or his army is never safe."

Hadrian's Wall and all its defenses took more than six years to build and cost the equivalent of hundreds of millions of dollars in today's money. About fifteen thousand soldiers were required to garrison the forts, milecastles, and watchtowers along the wall. Many of them came not from Rome, but from other parts of its empire. There were infantrymen from Greece, archers from Syria, and cavalrymen from northern France.

Occasionally a raiding party from the north would seize a watchtower or milecastle, burn its wooden furnishings, and destroy as much of the stonework as they could. But the raiders were invariably repulsed and the damage repaired. During the more than 250 years that Hadrian's Wall was actively defended, there is no evidence that any large portion of it was ever captured or held by an enemy.

The wall's collapse came about in a different way. During the last years of the fourth century A.D., the tribes to the north of the wall formed an alliance with the Scots in the west and the Saxons in the east. The wall's defenders might have been able to repel the combined forces of their enemies if the garrisons had been maintained at full strength. But many Roman soldiers had been transferred from Britain to fight more dangerous foes, like the Goths and the Persians, in the eastern part of the empire.

The remaining soldiers walled up the gateways in many of the forts and milecastles so that the wall would be easier to defend. When their numbers were reduced even further, the soldiers knew they could no longer hold the wall. Eventually the soldiers withdrew to the south of England. By 400 A.D. Hadrian's Wall was abandoned.

In the centuries that followed, the wall never again served as a fortification. But stones from it were put to many other uses by the English people who lived nearby. Some of the stones became the foundations and walls of churches; others were used in the construction of barns and houses; still others were cut into paving blocks for streets and roads.

In less populated areas, though, many sections of the wall remained much as they were in Roman times. Today a visitor can walk along these sections and look out at the rolling lands to the north, just as Roman sentries did almost sixteen hundred years ago.

THE GREAT WALL OF CHINA

Turn-of-the-century Chinese peasants looking down from the Great Wall (The Library of Congress)

When Hadrian's Wall was new, another wall already stretched across a vast country on the other side of the world. This rampart is the longest structure ever built. It contains enough building materials to circle the entire globe at the equator with a wall eight feet high and three feet thick. It is the only man-made structure on earth that can be seen with the naked eye from the moon. It is the Great Wall of China.

The Great Wall extends across northern and central China from the Yellow Sea in the east to a point deep in central Asia. There are different estimates of its overall length. Those who count only its distance east to west say it is approximately sixteen hundred miles long. Others claim that, with all of its loops and offshoots included, the wall is more than thirty-six hundred miles long. If straightened, they say, it would cross the United States from New York City to San Francisco, and there would be enough left over to wind back to Salt Lake City.

Construction of the wall spread over almost two thousand years, from 400 B.C., when the first sections were erected, until the 1600s A.D., when it was rebuilt and extended. But most of the wall was built in the ten years between 224 and 214 B.C. by Emperor Shih Huang-ti.

Shih was the first ruler to unify the scattered city states of China into a single nation. He accomplished this by a ruthless use of force. Like Adolf Hitler in the twentieth century, Shih ordered the burning of books he disagreed with, especially the writings of the philosopher Confucius. When some scholars continued to teach from these books, Shih had the scholars buried alive as an example to others who might think of disobeying him.

So that people and goods could travel easily from one part of China to another, Shih embarked on a vast road- and canal-building program. And to protect his new nation from northern invaders, Shih launched his most ambitious project — the linking of many smaller, older walls into one great defensive wall.

Such a wall was badly needed. For years the Tartars and other nomadic tribes had swept across the loosely defended border and attacked Chinese living in settled communities. The nomads looted Chinese homes, shops, and temples, burned the settlements to the ground, killed most of the men and children, and carried off some of the women as slaves.

The nomads laid siege to larger cities, too. Sometimes the inhabitants managed to hold out for a few weeks behind their city's walls. But unless an army garrison came to relieve them, the city dwellers were usually forced by hunger and disease to surrender. Then the looting, burning, and killing began all over again.

To prevent such terrible raids and bring hope to Chinese living on the border, Emperor Shih made construction of the Great Wall his first priority. He assigned an army of three hundred thousand men under one of his best

Sixteenth-century Italian drawing showing an elephant coming through a gate in the Great Wall (The New York Public Library)

generals, Meng Tien, to work on the project. Local laborers were recruited to assist the soldiers. Among them were thousands of women, who were hired to weave tents and help to carry loads.

Some of the hardest jobs were given to prisoners who were sent to the construction sites under armed guard. Besides common criminals, these prisoners included many people who had been captured in war or arrested for political reasons.

Historians estimate that all told more than a million people worked on the Great Wall. They labored from dawn to dusk, in freezing winter blizzards and blinding summer sandstorms. Clay for bricks was carried in baskets at the ends of shoulder poles. Building stones often had to be transported for long distances on crude sledges or wagons. In mountainous areas, the stones were sometimes raised into position by teams of specially trained goats.

Most of the workers suffered under harsh living conditions. Food rations frequently ran short and wells dried up. Flimsy tents offered little protection from blazing summer heat or sub-zero winter temperatures. Another problem was surprise attacks by nomadic enemy tribes. Often the soldiers in General Meng's army had to stop work in order to protect the other laborers.

As a result of all this, according to some Chinese historians, more than four hundred thousand men and women died while working on the wall. That was almost half the total work force. Many of the dead were buried within the wall, causing some people to call it "the longest cemetery in the world."

Reports of the human suffering along the wall inspired Chinese storytellers to create myths and legends. One of the best known centered on a princess from a captured city-state whose husband was sent to work on the wall. Like countless others he died and was buried in it.

After overcoming her grief, the princess set out for the wall to find her husband's body. No one could tell her where it was among the thousands of other corpses. The princess was about to give up the search when a spirit suddenly appeared before her.

"Cut your finger and hold it in front of you," the spirit said. "Follow where the blood falls. There you will find your husband's body."

Having spoken, the spirit vanished.

The princess was startled, but she followed the spirit's instructions. After a time the trail of her blood led her, as if by magic, to a gap in the wall where she found her husband's corpse. She took it back to her native city and reburied it with all the proper ceremonies.

At last, after more than ten years, the Great Wall was completed. Its thirty-five-hundred-mile route ran across plains and deserts, bridged ravines and rivers, and climbed over mountains as high as six thousand feet above sea level.

The wall was generally twenty-five feet wide at the base, slanting to seventeen feet at the top. It was between twenty-five and thirty feet high. In eastern China, where rocks were plentiful, the sides were faced with large stones or granite boulders, and the top was paved with bricks. The interior was composed of small stones and earth, cemented with a mortar so hard that nails couldn't be driven into it.

Five-foot-high stone parapets rose on both sides of the wall's flat top.

OVERLEAF: *The Great Wall winding through the mountains*
(Hsinhua News Agency)

The parapets had openings at regular intervals through which arrows could be shot at attackers. The top itself served as a road, wide enough for eight people to walk abreast, or two horse-drawn chariots to pass each other.

Farther west, the wall crossed barren deserts where stones were scarce. In those sectors it was constructed of earth alone. The builders moistened the earth with water carried from distant wells, and pounded it to make it solid.

Every few hundred yards along the wall, a watchtower rose about twelve feet above the walkway. These towers were manned by small groups of soldiers and served as lookout posts. If the soldiers saw a hostile band approaching the wall, they sent up a signal — smoke during the day, colored lights at night. The lights came from blazing logs that were coated with metal oxides to produce different colors. A red light meant danger, a blue one signified that all was quiet.

There were also many larger *garrison towers,* or forts, along the wall. Each of these could hold between one hundred and two hundred soldiers with their weapons, ammunition, and provisions. When a danger signal sent from a watchtower was seen at one of the garrison towers, the soldiers stationed there raced along the top of the wall to the spot that was threatened.

The entire wall was probably not garrisoned at any given time; that would have required many millions of soldiers. But historians estimate that in the days of Shih Huang-ti an army of perhaps a million men guarded the rampart.

For centuries the Great Wall protected northern China against small-scale attacks. But gradually the number of troops manning it was reduced, and large sections fell into ruin. In 1211 A.D. it proved no barrier to the Mongol leader Genghis Khan. He and his horse soldiers broke through the wall's defenses and conquered much of China.

The Mongols were driven out of China in the late 1300s and the wall was rebuilt. Frontier defense forces patrolled its fortifications from Manchuria in the east to Kansu in the west, and kept China largely free of Mongol raiders.

As the military threat from the north lessened, much of the wall was abandoned again. People living nearby started chipping away at it and removing stones to use in building houses and temples. Over time, long stretches of the wall — especially those made of earth — simply crumbled into dust. Other sections remained intact, however. During the war with Japan in the 1930s, Chinese soldiers marched to the northern front along the ancient brick road atop the wall.

After the Chinese Communists took power in 1949, several sections of the wall were restored once more — not as a military fortification but as a historical monument. Today the Communists point to the wall with

Watchtowers along the Great Wall
(The Library of Congress)

pride, saying that "it embodies the wisdom and blood and sweat of the Chinese working people." The restored section north of Peking has become a major tourist attraction, visited each year by thousands of people from all over the world.

It takes two hours to reach this restored section by train or bus. Suddenly, craggy mountains loom into view above the plain, and then the wall itself appears, curving over and around the mountains like a giant stone snake.

From the parking lot, steep inclines lead up to watchtowers at both ends of the restored section. It's a hard climb, but the view from the towers is worth the effort. Gazing out at the wall as it winds away across the mountains, one can't help but be amazed at the simple fact that it's there.

Besides its appeal as a tourist attraction, the wall is being used in other ways today. Scientists study it to learn the effects of earthquakes that occurred in the past. Archaeologists dig in and around it in search of tools and other objects from the time when it was built.

And previously unknown sections are still being discovered. In 1983 archaeologists unearthed a sixty-two-mile segment, thus adding to the already incredible length of the Great Wall of China — truly one of the wonders of the world.

·6·

CASTLE WALLS

A reconstructed English motte-and-bailey castle (The New York Public Library)

From a distance, the palisade of sharpened wooden logs looks as if it is encircling the top of a hill. But when you get closer you realize that the hill is a huge man-made mound, seventy-five to one hundred feet high, and one hundred to three hundred feet in diameter.

A deep, water-filled ditch surrounds the mound. On the other side of the ditch is a semicircular area of two or three acres that is also protected by a palisade and a ditch. A narrow bridge extends across the outermost ditch to a gate in the lower palisade. Another bridge stretches upward from the lower level to a fortified gate in the palisade around the mound. There are no other entrances to either enclosure.

This is a typical motte-and-bailey castle. "Motte" in old French meant hill or mound, and "bailey" was the word for the fenced-in area that stood in front of the motte. Castle came from the Latin word "castellum," meaning a fortified dwelling house.

Behind the palisade atop the motte rises a two- or three-story watch-tower, known as a *keep*. The keep in a motte-and-bailey castle often included living quarters on the lower floors. The bailey usually contained additional living quarters, a stable for horses, barns for cattle, and storehouses for grain and other foods. There also had to be a well or spring within the walls to assure a supply of fresh water in case the castle was besieged.

Starting in the ninth century, local lords built motte-and-bailey castles in France and other European countries. They served as private fortresses from which a lord could govern the territory he controlled and to which he could retreat if another lord attacked him. When William of Normandy conquered England in 1066, he brought the idea of the motte-and-bailey castle with him. Within a short time such castles guarded key points along the English coast and the borders with Wales and Scotland.

Motte-and-bailey castles had several strong points. They could be erected quickly — sometimes within as little as two or three weeks — and did not require skilled craftsmen. Often local labor was employed. The writers of the *Anglo-Saxon Chronicle* described this in bitter tones: "They [the Normans] burdened the unhappy people of the country with forced labor on the castles; and when they were built they filled them with wicked men."

The castles could be defended quite easily, too. If the outer bailey was occupied, the defenders climbed up to the motte, destroying the single bridge behind them. There they could hold out for quite a long while if they had sufficient food and water. The steepness of the motte's sides, coupled with the palisade at the top, made a direct assault almost impossible.

The chief weakness of motte-and-bailey castles was their timberwork. Often a castle's defenders were forced to surrender when an enemy set fire to the keep and palisade with flaming arrows. Even if the castle successfully

The Tower of London (Southend Air Photography, Ltd.)

withstood a siege, its wooden walls would eventually rot and have to be replaced.

To solve this problem, English castle builders began to use stone instead of wood in the walls of their structures. By the early twelfth century, two types of stone castles had made their appearance in England: the *square keep* and the *shell keep*. Both types were often erected on the sites of old motte-and-bailey castles.

The Tower of London was probably the best-known of the square keeps. Begun by William of Normandy — otherwise known as William the Conqueror — and completed by his successor, the tower rose to a height of ninety feet and had walls that were between twelve and fifteen feet thick. It was designed to provide strong and secure accommodation for the king, his family, his treasure, and the principal members of his household. The tower also served as the model for all the square stone keeps that were built throughout England in the twelfth and thirteenth centuries.

Most of these square, or tower, keeps were placed in the baileys of old castles rather than on the mottes, because the piled-up earth of the mottes usually wasn't strong enough to support the keeps' heavy stone construction. The walls of some tower keeps were as much as twenty feet thick.

The top of a tower keep usually had four turrets, one at each corner. A walkway with a protective parapet along one side linked the turrets. There were openings for archers to shoot through in the walls of the turrets as well as the parapet.

Later in the twelfth century, outer stone walls were built around some tower keeps to give them added protection. These walls often contained towers at the corners and other key spots. Eventually the Tower of London was surrounded by a wall that included no less than a dozen smaller towers.

While the baileys of many old castles became tower keeps, the wooden palisades around the mottes in many other castles were replaced with cir-

Air view of Restormel, an English castle with a shell keep (Royal Commission on Historical Monuments [England])

cular stone walls. Such walls, together with the buildings inside them, were known as shell keeps.

In most shell keeps, the living quarters and storehouses were built directly against the wall to help reinforce it. Little light reached these rooms because there were usually few if any windows in the wall. The outer walls of shell keeps were often ten to twelve feet thick and sat on stone foundations sunk six or seven feet into tightly packed earth. The height of the walls varied from fifteen to thirty feet.

As on the walls of tower keeps, a walk usually ran around the top of a shell keep's wall. The walk was reached by a stairway within the wall and had a parapet, called a *battlement,* behind which the defenders could crouch in case of an attack.

Rounded towers were located at regular intervals along the walls of many shell keeps to give them additional strength. Heavy doors opened out from the towers onto the wall walks on either side of the tower. If an enemy captured a section of the walk, the tower doors were immediately sealed, cutting off the enemy soldiers and transforming the towers into independent fortresses.

The siege methods and weapons that an attacking force used against castle walls were much the same as those that enemy armies had been employing against city walls for more than two thousand years. In order to get into the inner courtyard and seize the keep, the attackers tried to break through the outer defensive wall with battering rams, climb over it with ladders, or undermine it by digging tunnels.

The methods the defenders used were much the same, too. They dug deep moats around their castles to make it harder for an attacker to bring his battering rams into position. They built the walls higher so he wouldn't be able to scale them with even the tallest ladders, and they thickened the bases in order to resist his mining attempts.

Like the Babylonians and Hebrews of ancient times, the defending soldiers also stood behind their stone battlements and aimed arrows or rocks down at the attackers. Most battlements had alternating high and low sections, like teeth with gaps between them. The high sections, called *merlons,* contained narrow slits through which arrows could be fired. The lower sections, called *embrasures,* were wide enough so that the defenders could drop rocks over them onto the enemy, then duck down behind the battlement for protection against the enemy's arrows.

British castle builders introduced some new defensive techniques, too. For instance, they slanted outward the bottom of the wall in many castles. The slant made an excellent springboard from which rocks hurled down from above could be bounced out at the enemy.

The builders also perfected defensive structures called *hoardings.* These

Dropping rocks and boiling oil through a hoarding

were wooden platforms that projected outward at right angles from the battlements. The hoardings were supported by wooden beams that fitted into holes in the castle's walls, and they usually had slanted roofs covered with shingles or hides, and wooden side walls. In their floors were holes through which stones and boiling liquids could be thrown on the heads of attackers.

Wooden hoardings had several serious drawbacks, however. Heavy stones from a catapult or mangonel could pierce their roofs or sides and wound the defenders. Or the hoarding might be set on fire by a flaming arrow shot from below. These problems weren't overcome until the thirteenth century, when British castle builders began to construct hoardings made of stone. They were called *machicolations,* which had always been the word for the holes in the floor through which stones were dropped.

Despite the new defensive measures, besiegers still found ways to conquer a castle. Sometimes they did so by making use of the toilets, or *garderobes,* which were built into a castle's wall at various levels. These

Ruins of Gaillard Castle (French Government Tourist Office)

small stone chambers contained drains that ran down through the wall to a cesspit below. In some castles, the drains emptied directly into the moat. When Gaillard Castle in France was besieged in 1204, the attackers managed to climb up through the drains and catch the castle's defenders off guard.

Castles in England reached their highest point of development at the end of the twelfth century. It was then that King Edward I, having put down a series of rebellions in Wales, decided to embark on a massive castle-building program. He had made Wales a principality of England — ever since, the heir to the British throne has been known as the Prince of Wales — and he needed a string of powerful castles from which to rule the region.

Thousands of craftsmen came from all over England and western Europe to help construct the eight castles in the king's plan. The equivalent of more than $10 million was spent to make sure that their walls and other defenses incorporated all the latest features in castle design.

Several of them were what was known as concentric castles. This meant that they had not just one defensive wall around them, but two. At Rhuddlan Castle, the inner bailey, or *ward,* was bounded by a stone wall

The concentric walls of Rhuddlan Castle, as seen from the moat (The British Tourist Authority)

Beaumaris, one of the concentric castles built by King Edward I
(The Welsh Office)

nine feet thick and thirty feet high, with battlements at the top. Fifty feet beyond this inner wall rose a second one half the height of the first. The outer wall also had battlements at the top, as well as narrow slits along its sides through which arrows could be shot.

Immediately outside the second wall of Rhuddlan Castle stretched a wide, dry ditch with steeply slanted sides. Because of the double walls, the ditch and the flat land beyond it could be covered with artillery fire from three different levels: the battlements on both the walls and the arrow slits in the outer one. The concentric walls of Rhuddlan Castle presented a formidable obstacle to any attacker, and they were never successfully breached.

Since they offered the only openings to the outside world, *gatehouses* received special attention in King Edward's castles. The King's Gate in the wall of Caernarvon Castle was without doubt the largest and most impressive of all.

Anyone approaching the King's Gate first had to cross a drawbridge over the moat. In times of danger the drawbridge could be raised on pulleys to form an additional barrier to the castle.

Before going through the outer gates, the visitor passed under the first *portcullis*. This was a wooden grille faced with iron, and with iron spikes all across the bottom. Men stationed in a room above the gate operated the portcullis by means of ropes or chains. It moved up and down in stone grooves at either side of the gate.

A portcullis

Caernarvon Castle from the air. The King's Gate is at center left. (The Welsh Office)

When the thick, heavy outer doors of the King's Gate were opened to the visitor, he did not immediately enter the bailey or courtyard of the castle. Instead he found himself in an inner chamber facing another portcullis and another gate beyond it. In the stone walls on either side were narrow peepholes through which he could be watched, and in the ceiling above there was a large opening through which objects could be dropped down on him if he made any suspicious moves.

All told there were five such chambers, portcullises, and gates through and under which any visitor to Caernarvon had to pass before he finally gained admission to the castle proper. And all of the chambers were equipped with arrow slits and peepholes in their side walls, and "murder holes" in their ceilings.

Perhaps because of these elaborate defenses, Caernarvon Castle was never captured, although it was attacked and severely damaged in 1294 by the Welsh chieftain Madog, when it was only half completed. Later, in 1404, it was besieged unsuccessfully by another Welsh leader, Owen Glendower.

When the famous British writer Dr. Samuel Johnson visited Caernarvon in 1774, he is reported to have exclaimed: "I did not think there had been such buildings, such gates. They surpassed all my ideas." Tourists today, more than two hundred years later, still stand in awe before the castle's walls and the King's Gate.

The walls of Caernarvon Castle (The British Tourist Authority)

Castle building wasn't limited to western Europe. Regional lords built distinctive castles in Japan, too, starting in the 1100s and continuing through the early 1600s.

Himeji Castle, located eighty miles southwest of the city of Kyoto, is typical of Japanese castle construction at its height. It was built between 1601 and 1609 by the trusted son-in-law of the ruling shogun as a defense against the lords of western Japan who were trying to overthrow the shogun.

The castle is situated on top of a hill and is surrounded by a deep moat. Like all Japanese hill castles, Himeji has a massive foundation made of huge, tightly fitted stones. From this foundation rise walls of wood,

OPPOSITE: *The walls of Himeji Castle, covered with fireproof plaster* (Japan National Tourist Organization)
BELOW: *Himeji Castle, with the five-story donjon at its core* (Japan National Tourist Organization)

Path to the donjon of Himeji Castle (Japan National Tourist Organization)

covered with layer upon layer of fireproof white plaster. The walls are topped with black clay tiles.

A five-story central *donjon*, or keep, towers above the walls. Each of the donjon's white-walled stories is smaller than the one beneath it, and the eaves are tiled like the walls. Because it resembled a great white bird in flight, the Japanese nicknamed Himeji "White Heron Castle."

As in King Edward's Welsh castles, elaborate precautions were taken to make entering Himeji Castle as difficult as possible. The main path leading from the outer gate of the castle to its central donjon has many twists and turns, and is interrupted by no fewer than twenty-one gates. In front of each gate the path narrows so that only a few people can get through at any one time. And all along the path there are openings in the walls on either side through which the defenders could take aim at an enemy.

Protected by defenses like these, the inner citadels of Japanese castles were almost never penetrated. If an enemy did manage to break through the maze of paths and walls, the lord of the castle usually committed suicide rather than surrender. Often he would destroy his donjon by setting it afire at the same time as he killed himself. Many Japanese castles, including Himeji, were equipped with piles of straw for use as kindling if such a situation arose.

As the central government of Japan grew more powerful during the 1600s, Japanese castles ceased to be military bases. Much the same thing occurred at an earlier date in Europe. In England, for example, the strong government of the Tudor kings, combined with the end of fighting in Wales in the 1400s, did much to reduce the need for castles.

Even if this hadn't happened, another development had made castle walls obsolete. That was the invention of cannons using gunpowder. By the mid-1400s, the artillery of King Charles VII of France was so effective that, in his campaign to drive the English out of Normandy, the king battered down the walls of sixty castles in a single year.

After that, castles became mere residences and people started to build a new kind of defensive wall — one that could stand up against cannon fire.

7

WALLS TO WITHSTAND ARTILLERY

An early cannon; etching on iron by Albrecht Dürer (The Metropolitan Museum of Art, Fletcher Fund, 1919)

The new cannons struck fear in the hearts of fifteenth-century soldiers standing atop the high walls of cities and castles. The earliest examples of these weapons, called *bombards,* were simple tubes of cast or wrought iron, and they were used almost exclusively in siege operations. They had to be moved about on ox-drawn sledges and set on mounds of earth or log platforms for firing. Only later were the *tubes,* or barrels, of the guns placed on wheeled frames called *carriages.*

The projectiles these early cannons fired were balls of iron or stone that contained no explosives of their own. First a charge of powder was pushed to the bottom of the barrel, followed by a wad of cloth to help ignite the charge, and finally by the projectile, or *shot.* Then the gunner applied a flaming stick to a narrow vent in the barrel that led to the gunpowder. The powder exploded, propelling the shot out of the barrel with tremendous force.

Some fifteenth-century cannons were incredibly huge. The Turks used one in the siege of Constantinople in 1453 that weighed nineteen tons and fired stone balls of as much as fifteen hundred pounds for a distance of over a mile. It took a squad of soldiers, using pulleys and levers, to load this cannon.

No masonry walls built in the old style could hold up for long against such weapons. To meet their challenge, new fortifications had to be designed that could take the brunt of the enemy's cannon fire while delivering effective counterblows. All across Europe the rulers of countries and regions sought answers to this problem, and many talented individuals responded to their calls.

The great Italian artist and scientist Leonardo da Vinci suggested that the walls of fortresses be made lower but more heavily fortified. He drew plans for thick walls with three tiers of artillery to increase firepower. The cannons would be set in masonry emplacements called *casemates,* and fired through openings in the walls. The entire fortification would be circular in shape, and would be topped not with battlements, but with a giant dome called a *cupola.* The cupola form would help to deflect enemy shot and protect the soldiers stationed in the fortress.

The German artist Albrecht Dürer proposed building city walls flanked by tall, circular artillery towers and surrounded by a one-hundred-foot-wide ditch. Cannons would be mounted at the top of the towers for firing on an enemy at a distance. If the enemy soldiers got closer, other cannons positioned in casemates lower down in the tower could fire on them across the broad ditch and prevent them from crossing it.

The main problem with ideas like Da Vinci's and Dürer's was that their planned fortresses were too big and elaborate to construct economically. While waiting for a less expensive solution to emerge, most military

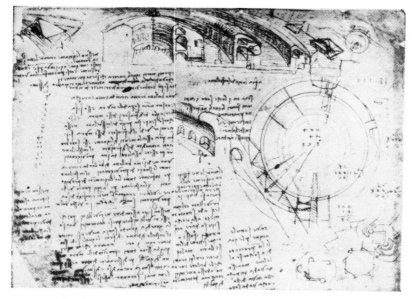

ABOVE: *Sketch of a fortification by Leonardo da Vinci* (The New York Public Library)
BELOW: Siege of a Fortress; *woodcut by Albrecht Dürer* (The Cleveland Museum of Art, Purchase, Dudley P. Allen Fund)

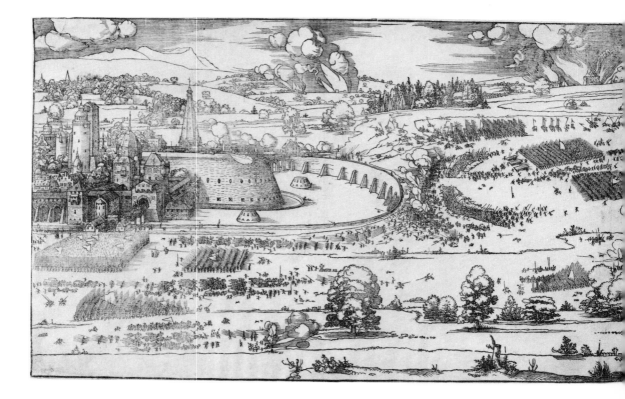

men simply lowered and thickened the existing walls around castles and cities so that they could support the weight of cannons. Then, in the mid-1500s, Italian engineers invented a new type of defensive wall that would eventually be used in fortifications all over the world. This was the *bastion*.

A bastion was triangular in shape and its point jutted out like an arrowhead from the walls of the fortress. The two flanks of a bastion were faced with stone or brick, and cannons were set behind embrasures along both sides. In this way, any approaching enemy would be caught in the cross fire from two neighboring bastions.

Most of the new-style forts had five or six such bastions, all pointing outward. This led to their being called "star fortresses." Unlike the old city and castle walls, the walls of bastioned fortresses rarely rose more than ten or twelve feet above the ground.

The defenses of the new forts started behind the bastioned walls and extended far beyond them. In the center of the fort, on ground level, stretched the *parade*. Next, on a higher level that encircled the parade like a terrace, came the *terreplein*. The fort's cannons were usually positioned on the terreplein, and it was surrounded by the bastioned wall, called a *parapet* like the top of castle and city walls.

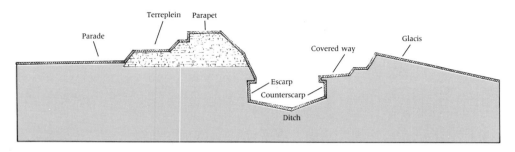

Cutaway view of the parts of a fortress

From the base of the parapet an earthen rampart gradually sloped down to a wide ditch or moat. The masonry wall of the ditch on the fort side was called the *escarp* and the wall on the far side the *counterscarp.* Halfway up the counterscarp there was often a path or road called the *covered way.* Soldiers standing on the covered way were protected by the top of the counterscarp while they defended the approaches to the fort with small firearms or light artillery.

The earth excavated from the ditch was spread in front of the counterscarp to form a gradually descending ramp called a *glacis.* The glacis helped to strengthen the counterscarp and the fort itself by absorbing many of the projectiles fired from the enemy's artillery. Cannonballs simply sank into an earthen rampart, whereas they tended to shatter a wall made of brick or stone.

If possible, the area around a fort and its glacis was cleared for at least three hundred yards of all rocks, bushes, and trees behind which an enemy might take cover. A cleared area also made it more difficult for the enemy to bring up his heavy artillery within range of the fort.

The living quarters for a fort's defending troops were often located under the terreplein. From them, tunnels led down through the earthen rampart to openings in the wall of the escarp. Soldiers stationed behind these openings could fire across the ditch at any attackers who gained control of the glacis and covered way.

Because bastioned forts had such a large circumference, and cost so much to build, they were erected only at the most important strategic locations. They guarded cities and trade routes, borders and seacoasts.

As artillery became more powerful in the 1600s, and their ranges greater, new and stronger fortifications had to be developed. In many fortresses a second masonry wall, known as a *tenaille trace,* was erected in front of the bastioned wall.

The tenaille trace consisted of a series of sharp triangular points called *redans,* which were linked together at right angles to form a continuous saw-toothed wall. From positions along the sides of each redan, musketeers could rake the ditch and glacis of the fortress with deadly cross fire.

By the late 1600s, the huge cost of fortifications — not to mention the high price of guns and ammunition — had drastically changed the nature of warfare. No longer was it a matter of petty quarrels between neighboring barons or lords. Now only the rulers of powerful nations or states could afford to go to war.

As this change in warfare occurred, a new profession came into being in Western Europe: military engineering. France soon took the lead in the field due to the work of such brilliant engineers as Sébastien de Vauban.

Born in 1633, Vauban received a cadetship in the French army when he was eighteen and began to lay out field fortifications two years later. His work came to the attention of King Louis XIV, and as a result, Vauban was made an "Engineer of the King" when he was only twenty-one.

Vauban once said, "The art of fortifying does not consist of rules and systems, but solely of good sense and experience." During France's wars with Holland and other countries, he had the opportunity to test his ideas of both siegecraft and fortification.

Before Vauban's time, when an attacking army besieged a fortress they usually dug a single trench around it and placed their artillery at the point closest to the fortification. Then they battered the bastioned wall with cannonballs until they managed to breach a hole in it. After that was accomplished, the attacking soldiers rushed forward, dodging musket and light artillery fire along the way. Often they were driven back time after time, with a great loss of men and equipment.

In place of this technique, Vauban devised a system of parallel trenches around a fortress, starting some six hundred yards back from it. That distance was the farthermost range of most artillery at the time. From the first trench, working at night, the attackers dug a number of zigzag trenches forward. These trenches were called *saps,* and the men who dug them were known as *sappers.* When all the saps had reached about halfway to the fortification, the sappers linked the outermost points in a new parallel trench. They piled up earthworks in front of it and brought up their muskets and artillery.

If the fortress didn't fall as a result of blows delivered from the second parallel trench, the sappers once again dug forward under cover of darkness until they reached the foot of the glacis. Then, working carefully to avoid the enemy's fire, they encircled the glacis with a third parallel trench.

After the heavy artillery was brought up to the third trench, it usually wasn't long before the guns opened up a breach in the rampart. As soon as that happened, the attackers swept down onto the covered way, seized it, raced across the ditch, and mounted the rampart with the aid of scaling ladders. This was the most dangerous part of the operation. In one of

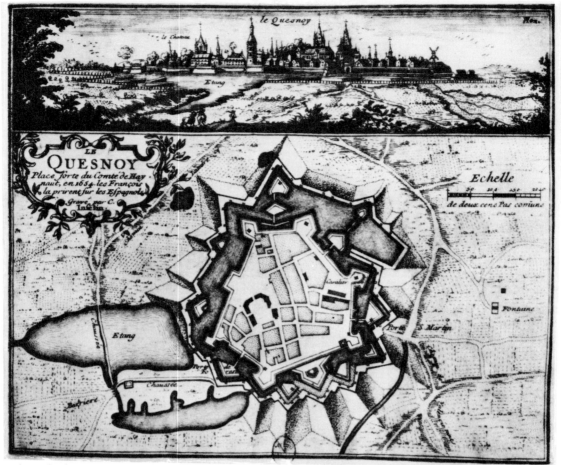

Plan of a bastioned fortification designed by Sébastien de Vauban
(The New York Public Library)

Vauban's sieges, twelve hundred men were killed by musket fire from the remaining bastions as they attempted to cross the ditch.

Usually, according to Vauban's schedule, the assault on the fortress itself began no more than twenty days after the first of the parallel trenches was dug. This was amazingly fast in comparison with sieges where the old methods of trenching were employed. They had often dragged on for months, with many more soldiers killed and wounded on both sides.

As a defender, Vauban designed fortifications that would stand up against the sort of siege techniques he himself had invented. He once summed up his theories in one short paragraph. ''Fortification, or military architecture,'' he said, ''is no other thing than an art, which teaches men how to fortify themselves with ramparts, parapets, moats, covered ways, and glacis, so that the enemy may not be able to attack such a part without great loss of his men; and so that the small number of soldiers who defend the place may be able to hold out for some time.''

In his fortifications, Vauban followed the traditional layout of a bastioned fortress but extended it as far as possible so that an attacker would have to begin siege operations at a greater distance.

Along with a bastioned wall and tenaille trace, the ditch played an important part in Vauban's fortifications. It was generally fifteen to thirty feet deep and as much as seventy-two feet wide, and was often filled with water drawn from a nearby stream or river.

In the middle of the ditch rose a number of triangular man-made islands called *ravelins*. The ravelins all pointed out toward the covered way and the glacis, and had openings in their sides through which muskets were fired. Tunnels led from the rampart, under the ditch, and up to the ravelins so that soldiers could move freely from one part of the fortress to another.

Like the outer walls in concentric castles, the main purpose of the ravelins was to serve as yet another barrier to the main wall of the fortress. Their walls were lower than those of the tenaille trace and the bastions behind them so that if any of the ravelins were captured by an enemy, they would still be vulnerable to fire from the walls to the rear.

Vauban's new ideas for defense didn't stop with the ravelins. He topped the escarp wall of the ditch with a *cordon*, a projecting layer of masonry that made climbing the slope of the rampart more difficult. And at the foot of the glacis, on the outer reaches of the fortification, he had pits dug to a depth of six or more feet and filled with sharpened stakes. Anyone trying to leap up onto the glacis ran the risk of falling into one of these pits and being impaled on a stake.

During his career, Sébastien de Vauban built or redesigned more than 160 fortresses. In recognition of his accomplishments, he was named a marshal of France in 1703, four years before his death. But his theories of fortification long outlived him. They dominated European military thinking until late in the nineteenth century. They also helped to shape American ideas of fortification after they were brought to the New World by French military men who had studied Vauban's methods.

8

WALLS OF AMERICAN FORTS

Fort Ticonderoga today (Fort Ticonderoga Museum)

One of the earliest and best examples of a French-style fort in North America is Fort Ticonderoga, which was called Fort Carillon when it was built in 1755 by French military engineers from Canada.

Located on the shores of Lake Champlain in what is today New York State, the fort commanded the vital water route between Canada and New York City. It helped to establish French control of the area, and served as a defense against possible attacks by British colonists from New England and raids by local Indian tribes.

Like many smaller forts in France and other European countries, Fort Carillon was square in plan, with four bastions at the corners. It contained room for a garrison of four hundred men.

Because the French had no stonemasons with them when they first arrived, they built the fort's walls of oak logs laid horizontally. There were actually two walls, set ten feet apart and joined by wooden crosspieces. The space between the walls was filled with earth to strengthen them against artillery shells. Eventually the French faced the outer surfaces of the wall with stone.

As an added protection for the fort's northern and western sides, the French erected two ravelins beyond the wall. Around the fortifications they blasted out a ditch from solid rock and built a covered way on its far side. The slope of the ridge on which the fort stood provided a natural glacis.

Fort Carillon changed hands many times over the years. The British captured it from the French in 1759 during the French and Indian War, and renamed it Fort Ticonderoga. At the start of the revolutionary war, in 1775, Ethan Allen and his Green Mountain Boys, from Vermont, seized it from the British in a surprise attack. However, a British army under General John Burgoyne recaptured the fort in 1777 and held it until the end of the Revolution.

In 1820 the abandoned fort and the surrounding lands were bought by a wealthy New York City merchant, William Pell. He built a house on the property and kept the fort from being dismantled by local farmers. One of Pell's descendants, Stephen Pell, decided to restore the fort to its original form in the early 1900s, and dedicated himself to the project. Standing within the bastioned walls today, many visitors feel as if they have been transported back to the eighteenth century.

Vauban's principles of fortification were also applied in the design of Fort McHenry, which was built between 1794 and 1805 to guard the harbor of Baltimore, Maryland.

Named for James McHenry, who was secretary of war at the time, Fort McHenry was a star-shaped fortress with five bastions for artillery. It

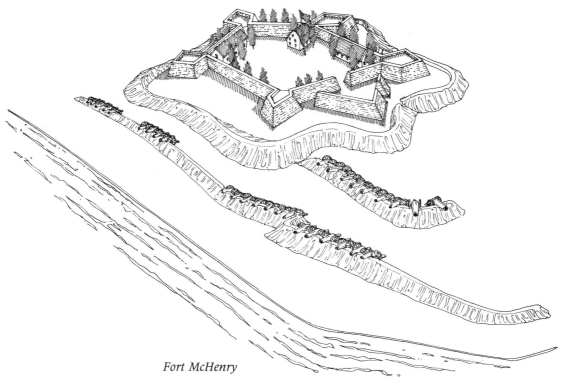

Fort McHenry

had one ravelin opposite the entrance to protect it, and a ditch all the way around the fortifications.

The walls of Fort McHenry met their severest test when a British fleet attacked Baltimore during the War of 1812. The British ships had guns with a longer range than those in the fort. The vessels stopped out of range of the American guns and let loose with a barrage of rockets and mortar shells. The mortars were especially dangerous; they were fired into the air at a forty-five degree angle so that their shells would land behind the walls of the fort. The Americans couldn't return the fire, but fortunately the fort's bastions withstood the attack, which went on all day.

That night the British tried to send several ships past the fort in order to land behind it. At last the Americans could shoot back, aiming at the flashes of the British ships' return fire. The British retreated, and Francis Scott Key, who had been watching the battle all night, wrote the lyric for ''The Star-Spangled Banner'' the next morning.

The American commander estimated that the British had fired as many as eighteen hundred shells at Fort McHenry during the bombardment, and that five hundred or more had landed within the fort's defenses. One gun had been disabled; two buildings had been damaged; four American soldiers had been killed and twenty-four wounded. But the strong walls and bastions of the fort remained intact.

After the War of 1812 was over, President James Madison ordered the construction of a number of forts up and down the Atlantic coast. Among them were Fort Pulaski, which guarded the approaches to Savannah, Georgia, and Fort Sumter, which protected the city of Charleston, South Carolina.

Fort Sumter and Fort Pulaski both had three tiers of guns, two of them set in casemates and the third positioned behind a parapet on top of the wall. With three tiers, the gunners could fire a lot of shots all at once and

Aerial view of Fort Pulaski (National Park Service, U.S. Department of the Interior)

ABOVE: *Guns atop the parapet of Fort Pulaski* (National Park Service, U.S. Department of the Interior, Photo by Cecil W. Stoughton)

LEFT: *Casemates at Fort Pulaski* (National Park Service, U.S. Department of the Interior, Photo by Cecil W. Stoughton)

OPPOSITE: *Fort Sumter before the Civil War* (The Library of Congress)

counter the guns on enemy ships, many of which had three gun decks of their own.

Both forts were intended as defenses against a possible attack by a foreign power. Instead, both of them played significant roles in the American Civil War (1861–1865). In fact, Fort Sumter was the place where the war began.

Construction of Fort Sumter, which was named for South Carolina's Revolutionary War patriot Thomas Sumter, began in 1829 but was not yet completed at the end of 1860 because of construction delays and insufficient financing. Situated on a shoal in Charleston harbor, the fort had the form of a pentagon, with a projecting angle that pointed out to sea. Its walls rose more than forty feet above the waters of the harbor and were five feet thick.

On December 20, 1860, South Carolina became the first of the southern states to secede from the United States over the slavery issue. Immediately the governor of South Carolina threatened to take control of all federal property in the state, including the major forts in Charleston harbor, Fort Moultrie and Fort Sumter.

Major Robert Anderson, commander of the federal garrison at Fort Moultrie, decided to move his men and equipment across the harbor to Fort Sumter. Even though Fort Sumter was still uncompleted, the major felt that its position, surrounded on all sides by water, would make it easier to defend if the South Carolinians carried out their threats to seize the fort.

Fort Sumter had been designed to accommodate a garrison of 650. No guns had yet been installed at the fort, but there were places for 135 of them in casemates along the walls and behind the parapet on top. Major Anderson's garrison of eighty-five men reached Sumter safely on the evening of December 26, 1860. They dispersed their sixty-five cannons as effectively as possible and bricked up the unused gun embrasures to strengthen the fort's walls. They knew, however, that the fort could only hold out so long without fresh reinforcements, supplies, and ammunition from the federal government in Washington.

In April 1861 the newly inaugurated President, Abraham Lincoln, decided to send a relief convoy backed up by warships to the aid of Fort Sumter. South Carolina and its southern allies responded by demanding that Major Anderson evacuate the fort at once. When he refused, southern guns opened up on Fort Sumter early in the morning of April 12. The Civil War had begun.

Although Major Anderson and his men returned the fire, they stood little chance against the army of seven thousand southerners that was lined up across the harbor. Shells tore big chunks out of the fort's southeast corner and set the wooden barracks on the parade ground on fire. The bombardment continued all day and resumed at dawn on the thirteenth. By midmorning, smoke filled the embrasures, choking the fort's gunners, and the flagstaff had been shot down.

Seeing that the U.S. flag was no longer flying over the fort, the southern general Pierre Beauregard sent a party to talk with Major Anderson. The major had orders not to fight to the last man to defend the fort. He realized that the situation was hopeless and agreed to surrender. Later that day, after Anderson and his men had left on a northern ship, the Confederate flag was raised over Fort Sumter.

Four thousand shells had been fired into the fort during the bombardment, but none of the eighty-five Union soldiers and officers had been killed. Fort Sumter's walls hadn't failed its defenders; its defenders had been defeated by a lack of men and supplies.

Events took a different course at Fort Pulaski. No federal troops were stationed there, so several detachments of Georgia militiamen simply occupied the fort in January 1861.

Fort Pulaski honored the memory of the Polish count Casimir Pulaski, who was killed in action while serving in Savannah as a volunteer with

The moat at Fort Pulaski (National Park Service, U.S. Department of the Interior, Photo by Cecil W. Stoughton)

the American army during the Revolution. Construction of the fort had begun in 1829, the same year Sumter was started. By 1847, when Fort Pulaski was completed, over $1 million had been spent on it and more than 25 million bricks had gone into its walls and buildings. Journalists claimed the fort was "as strong as the Rocky Mountains."

Like Fort Sumter, Fort Pulaski was a five-sided structure. Unlike Sumter, it was completely surrounded by a moat, seven feet deep and thirty-two to forty-eight feet in width. The fort's brick and masonry walls were seven-and-a-half feet thick and contained embrasures for 140 cannons.

Fort Pulaski had been designed for a garrison of 385 officers and men. It was fully manned by Confederate soldiers in November 1861 when federal troops from a blockading fleet captured Fort Walter on nearby Hilton Head

The parade at Fort Pulaski, looking toward the casemates in the walls (National Park Service, U.S. Department of the Interior, Photo by Cecil W. Stoughton)

Island. Determined to retake Fort Pulaski, the federal forces spent the next few months secretly hauling thirty-six cannons at night through thick mud to a point on Tybee Island just a mile from the walls of the fort. The soldiers finished the job on April 9, 1862, and began bombarding Fort Pulaski at eight o'clock the next morning.

The fort's thick walls proved to be no match for the new rifled cannons the federal troops fired at them. Cannons in the past had had smooth barrels on the inside. These new experimental cannons had spiraled, or rifled, grooves inside the barrel. When one was fired, a ring on the projectile engaged the rifling in the barrel, which provided a spin to the bullet-shaped shot.

This spin gave the projectile an accuracy, range, and power that could not be matched by the round shot of the old smoothbore artillery. Even at a distance of a mile, projectiles from the rifled cannons easily penetrated the walls of Fort Pulaski and sent bricks showering into the air.

Colonel Charles Olmstead, the Confederate commander of the fort, wrote his wife later: "It soon became evident to my mind that if the enemy continued to fire as they had begun that our walls must yield. Shot after shot . . . hit immediately about our embrasures. Some came through dismounting a gun, wounding one man very severely, and flaking off bricks in every direction."

The bombardment continued all that day, and resumed at eleven o'clock the next morning. By then the federal cannons had blasted completely through the walls of the fort's southeast corner and were crashing against the magazine, which contained forty thousand pounds of gunpowder. Rather than see his men blown up by their own ammunition, Colonel Olmstead surrendered just thirty hours after the bombardment had begun.

In the meantime, at Fort Sumter, Confederate troops had repaired the walls and filled the casemates with cannons in expectation of an attack by the Union navy. It came in April 1863, when nine of the North's new ironclads — warships covered with iron plates for protection — sailed past Fort Sumter with all guns blazing.

Although the barracks were set afire and two gun embrasures were destroyed, casualties in the fort were surprisingly light. The walls stood up well against the enemy fire and the fort's defenders sank one of the ironclads and disabled five others. The Union fleet withdrew from Charleston harbor and did not return the next day.

The North had not abandoned its goal of recapturing Fort Sumter, however. In July 1863, units of the Union army landed on an island across the harbor from the fort and fought their way to a position from which they could aim their new rifled cannons at its walls. Beginning in August 1863, the big Union guns pounded Fort Sumter day after day. And night after night General Beauregard's engineers made repairs, bricking up the casemates that had been destroyed and piling up heaps of earth behind the walls to help absorb the Union shells.

Eventually the side of the fort facing the Union guns was little more than a shapeless rampart of sand, earth, and shattered masonry, forty feet high and twenty-five feet thick. By the end of August, only one of Fort Sumter's cannons remained in action.

The Confederates managed to reinforce the fort's garrison under cover of night, though. As a result, a Union landing party of 450 men met with unexpected opposition when it tried to seize the fort in early September. Only 127 of the Union soldiers were able to get ashore, and all of them were captured, wounded, or killed by the Confederate defenders.

Interior of Fort Sumter after the bombardment (The Library of Congress)

By this time Fort Sumter had lost all meaning as a fortification, but it had become an important symbol of victory to both sides. The North was determined to recapture it as proof that it was winning the war, and the South was just as determined to hold on to it. The Confederate flag still flew over the fort and the one gun that was left fired a salute to it at sunset every night.

For eighteen more months Union guns continued to hurl shot after shot at the ruined fort while the defenders huddled in bombproof shelters deep underground. Historians later said that more than thirty-five hundred tons of ammunition struck Fort Sumter during those months.

The fort never did surrender. Instead, it was evacuated in February 1865, when the approach of the Union army under Major General William T. Sherman forced the evacuation of Charleston and the entire surrounding area.

The Union forces who took control of the fort found virtually nothing there except a huge mound of earth and rubble. The defenders of Sumter had held up bravely in the face of rifled cannons, but its walls — like those of Fort Pulaski — had collapsed under their blows.

Military observers in America and Europe studied what had happened at Fort Pulaski and Fort Sumter, and realized that the day of the bastioned masonry fort was over. Rifled artillery had made such forts obsolete, just as cannons had made castle walls obsolete four hundred years before.

Fort Sumter after the Civil War (The Library of Congress)

9

WALLS UNDERGROUND

Mougin's plan for an underground fort protected by cupolas

After the destruction of Fort Pulaski and Fort Sumter, military engineers decided that forts in the future would have to go underground. That was the only way their walls could escape the deadly blows of rifled artillery.

Several other weapons that were invented in the late nineteenth century made the need for stronger fortifications even more urgent. A machine gun was developed that could fire seven hundred rounds of ammunition a minute. Artillery pieces became larger and more powerful, and French engineers perfected an explosive shell.

All over Europe, architects and military engineers drew plans for forts that would meet the challenge of these new weapons in the event of war. In France, an engineer named Mougin published his ideas for an experimental fort in 1887. It was to be made of concrete, and most of the fort would be built deep in the ground. Nothing would be visible on the surface except for nine domelike steel cupolas.

The three larger cupolas provided cover for rifled artillery pieces. The guns sat on revolving bases, and there were openings in the cupolas through which they could be fired. Four smaller cupolas, each containing two machine guns, completed the fort's armament, while two other cupolas served as observation posts. The entrance to the fort was covered by a metal plate that could be raised or lowered hydraulically.

Down below the gun emplacements in Mougin's plan were chambers for ammunition and supplies, and living quarters for thirty or forty soldiers. A power plant at the base of the fort would generate the electricity required to light and ventilate it.

Mougin's fort was never actually built, but his ideas influenced other European military men as they remodeled old forts or built new ones in the last years of the nineteenth century.

Back in 1874, a circle of seventeen forts had been erected like a wall around the French city of Verdun. The forts were part of an overall plan to defend France's border with Germany. Most of the forts were five-sided, with ditches in front that were covered by guns set in thick concrete casemates. But French generals now feared these concrete walls wouldn't be able to stand up against blows from the Germans' big new guns.

Inspired by Mougin, the French engineers took the guns of the Verdun forts out of their casemates and reset them in steel cupolas that could be raised and lowered for firing. Then, remembering the lessons of Fort Sumter, they piled a three-foot layer of sand on the roof and sloping sides of each fort, and covered the sand with a layer of reinforced concrete. Reinforced concrete contained steel rods that made it much stronger than ordinary concrete.

Altogether the layered walls of the Verdun forts were more than ten feet thick. If all went as the engineers planned, any enemy shells that hit them would explode against the outer layer of reinforced concrete. Most of the shock of the explosion would be absorbed by the layer of sand beneath. And the men and guns within the forts would escape injury.

Belgian engineers in the late 1880s followed a more traditional plan when they built a wall-like ring of twelve forts around the city of Liège, near Belgium's border with Germany. Each of the forts was triangular in shape with a central concrete stronghold surmounted by eight revolving gun cupolas.

Surrounding the stronghold was a ditch. Its floor was filled with barbed wire, and in the middle stood an "unclimbable" concrete fence, ten feet tall and topped with sharp steel spikes. On the ditch's far side, as in Vauban's old forts, there was a covered way for riflemen, with a parapet over which they could fire their guns.

Beyond the ditch the earth sloped gradually downward. On this slope rose a number of smaller cupolas that contained light, quick-firing guns for close defense. Tunnels running under the ditch connected the covered way and the outer cupolas with the central stronghold.

When the German army invaded Belgium at the beginning of the First World War in 1914, it soon overran the Liège forts. The concrete surrounding the cupolas was too thin and weak to resist the Germans' heavy artillery. Many of the gun chambers crumbled, damaging the cupolas so that they could not be turned.

Besides this, living conditions proved intolerable for the three hundred to five hundred Belgian soldiers stationed in each fort. The ventilation systems often broke down, and some men were asphyxiated by poisonous fumes. Water cisterns cracked, and latrines overflowed.

Designed for the battle conditions of the 1880s, the Liège forts were no match for the German weapons of 1914. The last of the forts surrendered just eleven days after the attack began, and the Germans swept on into France.

There the Germans met their match in the huge French army, and the war quickly bogged down into a stalemate. Both sides dug themselves into lines of parallel trenches much like those that Vauban employed in his sieges. A stretch of battle-scarred earth called "No Man's Land" divided the two warring armies. Sometimes it was no more than a few hundred feet wide.

In many ways, the French and German trenches were the twentieth-century equivalent of the walls that guarded medieval cities and castles. There were usually three lines of trenches on each side of No Man's Land: the *front trench*, or *firing line*; the *support trench*, about two hundred and fifty to five hundred feet behind it; and the *reserve trench*, about five hundred

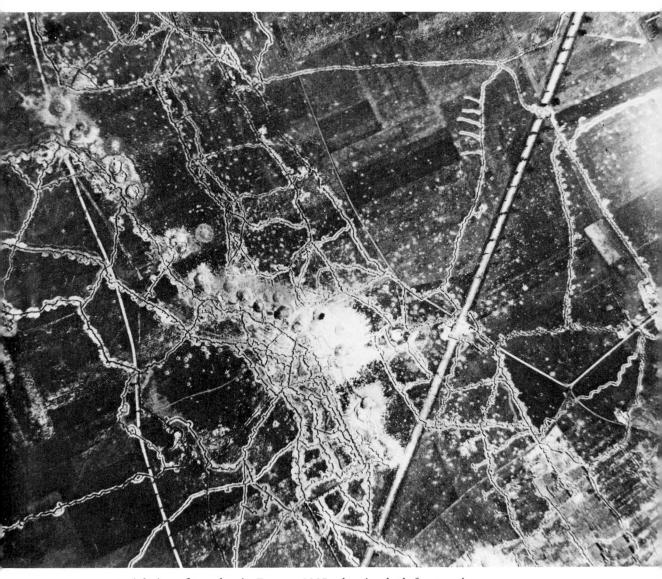

Aerial view of trenches in France, 1915, showing both front and support lines (Imperial War Museum)

to one thousand feet behind the second. Where possible, the reserve trench was dug on a rise of land so that it could command the entire scene with artillery fire.

Zigzag communications trenches, like Vauban's forward saps, linked the three lines. Along them, supplies and ammunition were moved forward, and the wounded were carried back to first-aid stations in the rear.

*British soldiers fixing their bayonets before going over the top of a
front-line trench* (Imperial War Museum)

Many sections of the trenches had side walls and roofs made of reinforced concrete. These sections were called *dugouts,* and the Germans constructed especially sturdy ones. The walls in front-line dugouts were usually
quite thin because the concrete had to be transported by hand from the
rear. Front-line dugouts were harder to build, too, because the men were
under almost constant enemy fire.

While most trench installations were better off below ground level,
some like machine-gun emplacements and lookouts had to be above it. If
there were farm buildings near the trenches, soldiers often took them over,
reinforced them with concrete, and installed machine guns in them. The
British made artificial tree trunks out of steel and set them up next to the
trenches to use as front-line observation posts.

For almost four years, from early 1915 to late 1918, the Allied and
German armies remained virtually frozen in their positions. The longer the
soldiers stayed in the trenches, the more heavily they fortified them. As a

result, the front-line dugouts became so solid that they were almost impossible to overrun. Hundreds of thousands of soldiers on both sides were killed or wounded in vain attempts to dislodge the enemy from his trenches.

Only in a few places on the western front did forts play an important role in the fighting. One of those places was Verdun. The layers the French had added to the walls of the Verdun forts in the 1880s proved their worth when the Germans attacked the city in full force in February 1916.

French soldiers standing in front of the entrance to one of the Verdun forts that withstood the German bombardment (Musée Memorial de Verdun)

Douaumont, one of the Verdun forts, after bombardment (Musée
Memorial de Verdun)

The Germans brought up their heaviest artillery, the guns known as
"Big Berthas." Each gun weighed over forty-two tons and had to be transported in sections on five railroad flatcars. It could be assembled in just a
few hours, though, using a light triangular hoist. The shell Big Bertha fired
weighed eighteen hundred pounds and had a range of 10,250 yards.

One of the seventeen Verdun forts fell quickly to the Germans, but
that was more because it was undermanned than because of Big Bertha.
The rest held out. Even Big Bertha's huge shells made little impression on
the massive concrete walls of the forts, cushioned by the layer of sand. The
shells shook the structures, and made an awful noise, but they failed to
penetrate the roofs or destroy the gun cupolas of specially hardened steel.
Almost all of the cupolas were still in good working order when Germany
surrendered over two years later in November 1918.

Because of the steady bombardment, life was anything but pleasant for the soldiers stationed in the Verdun forts. Most of them survived, though. So did the idea that walls, if they were thick enough and strong enough, could still play a decisive role in modern warfare. In fact the then President of France, Raymond Poincaré, said that it was the walls of Verdun "which broke the supreme hopes of Imperial Germany."

Ten years later the French remembered those words of Poincaré's when they were planning a new rampart against Germany — the elaborate defenses that came to be known as the Maginot line.

10

WALLS OF WORLD WAR II

Antitank defenses along the Maginot line (French Embassy Press and Information Center)

André Maginot, for whom the Maginot line was named, left his post as French undersecretary of state to enlist as a private in World War I. Although he was seriously wounded at Verdun, Maginot appreciated the strength of the city's fortifications and credited them with helping to save his life.

After the war, Maginot resumed his political career and by 1929 was the French minister of war. He didn't trust the Germans and believed that the only way to guard against their ambitions was to build a wall of powerful new fortifications along the border between France and Germany. The French Assembly agreed with Maginot, and in January 1930, voted to spend the equivalent of $36 million on the first phase of construction.

The Maginot line, as it soon came to be known, had to be completed by 1935. That was when French occupation forces were due to leave the Rhineland region of Germany, just across the border from France. This deadline had been spelled out in the Treaty of Versailles that ended World War I, and France wanted the new defenses to be ready by then.

Some thought the Maginot line would extend all the way from the Swiss Alps in the southeast of France to the English Channel in the northwest, but that was never the intention. The main strength of the line was concentrated along an eighty-seven-mile stretch of land in northeastern France. It consisted of what the French called "fortified regions," which guarded the two main possible invasion routes from Germany.

Journalists often referred to the Maginot line as the "Great Wall of France." Actually it was more like a giant version of Mougin's nineteenth century design for a fort.

Like the three lines of trenches in World War I, the fortifications of the Maginot line were arranged in rows that stretched back from the French frontier. In most places the fortified area was more than twelve miles deep. The defenses began with rows of antitank obstacles and thickets of barbed wire placed just behind the border. Backing them up were *maisons fortes*, or strong houses, small fortified barracks whose garrisons would sound the alarm of any enemy approach.

Next, about two miles to the rear, the French built *avant-postes*, or forward outposts. These were bunkers of thick reinforced concrete set in a hill or man-made mound. Each bunker was manned by a force of twenty-five to thirty-five soldiers armed with antitank and machine guns. Their job was to cover the approaches to the line and delay any enemy attack.

Several miles behind the *avant-postes* came the main fortifications of the region: the concrete casemates and the huge underground forts the French called *ouvrages*. Together these formed the backbone of the Maginot line.

The casemates all had two stories and were buried in a hill or mound

Concrete antitank obstacles on the Maginot line (Imperial War Museum)

like the *avant-postes*. Up to ten feet of earth and reinforced concrete shielded the roofs of the casemates from artillery shells and bombs.

Soldiers stationed in a casemate fired their antitank guns through openings in the top floor and slept in bunks on the floor below, where their ammunition and supplies were stored. Each casemate had its own diesel generator that provided electricity for lighting, ventilation, and to run the elevator that transported ammunition from the first floor to the second.

To protect the casemates against tanks, large tank traps were dug in front of them and filled with what the French called "asparagus beds." These consisted of rows of steel spikes, set at varying heights. An enemy tank that attempted to cross one of the traps would get stuck on the spikes. Antitank guns from a nearby casemate could then come into action and destroy the tank at point-blank range.

Some casemates were close enough to be connected by underground tunnels. All of them were linked by telephone with one another and with the great *ouvrages,* or forts. Like the forts along Hadrian's Wall and the

A casemate on the Maginot line (National Archives)

Great Wall of China, the *ouvrages* occurred at regular intervals; most of
them were four to six miles apart. The *ouvrages* received more publicity
than any other aspect of the Maginot line because nothing quite like them
had ever been built before.

The larger *ouvrages* could hold as many as twelve hundred soldiers.
They were divided into two groups of fortifications, both of which contained
between fifteen and eighteen concrete emplacements at the surface. Each
emplacement bristled with guns mounted in steel turrets that could be raised
and lowered. The guns ranged in size from machine guns and small antitank
guns to huge artillery pieces.

Beneath the surface, an *ouvrage* had many levels, like the decks of a
battleship or the basements and subbasements of an office building. Directly
below the gun emplacements were magazines for ammunition and living
quarters for the gun crews. From that level, elevators and stairways led
down to the command room, which was linked by intercom to the gun
positions and observation posts on the surface.

Gun emplacement of an
ouvrage *on the Maginot line*
(Hoover Institution)

Power station
in the Maginot line
(Imperial War Museum)

The elevators continued on down to the operations room and the four or five stories of barracks. Below the barracks, deep in the earth, was the power plant, which supplied the *ouvrage* with electricity. Also located on the lowest level were the kitchen, the hospital, and the main ammunition magazine. Water from deep-sunk wells filled reservoirs at the base of the *ouvrage,* and there were other reservoirs for fuel and lubricating oil.

Gradually sloping tunnels led from the heart of the *ouvrage* to the two main entrances on the surface. One was for personnel, the other for supplies. In case an enemy broke into a tunnel, it could be sealed at several points along the way by heavy armor-plated doors.

Railroad cars brought supplies up close to the rear of the line. From there a small electric train called the *metro* distributed them to different parts of the *ouvrage.* The *metro* ran on tracks through a tunnel that was only seven-and-a-half feet wide by nine feet high, and it transported troops as well as supplies.

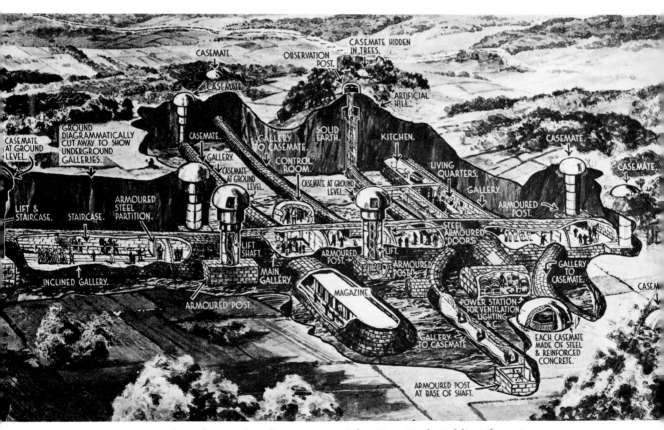

Cutaway view of a Maginot line ouvrage (The New York Public Library)

Transporting ammunition on the underground railway of a Maginot line ouvrage (National Archives)

  The *ouvrages* were like small, self-contained cities. Each one held enough supplies and ammunition so that it could survive for as long as three months if it were cut off from the rest of the French army.

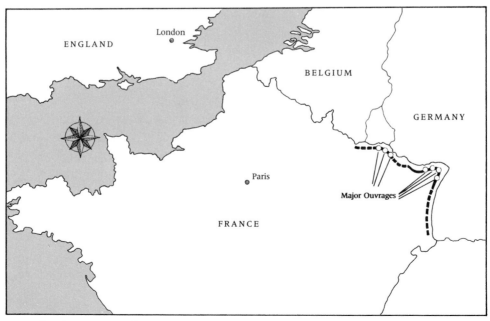

Map showing Maginot line

Early in 1936, soon after the main part of the Maginot line was completed, Germany reoccupied the Rhineland. According to the terms of the Locarno Pact, the Germans had agreed not to build any fortifications west of the Rhine River. However, the German leader Adolf Hitler violated the treaty and sent troops and warplanes into the Rhineland. France and Britain denounced his actions, and the League of Nations censured Germany. Hitler merely ignored their angry words and announced plans to build the West Wall — Germany's answer to the Maginot line.

Although some work was done on the West Wall in 1936 and 1937, most of it was built in just one year after Fritz Todt, Hitler's minister of armaments, took over command of the project in 1938.

The West Wall was planned to be over four hundred miles long and to run from Germany's border with Switzerland to the point where the Rhine enters the Netherlands. In most places it was composed of two zones: an Army Zone fifteen to twenty-five miles deep, and behind it an Air Defense Zone of twenty-five to forty miles. The German ministry of propaganda boasted that the West Wall was both longer and deeper than the Maginot line, which faced it.

Hitler intended the West Wall to frighten France and Britain and keep them from coming to the aid of two friendly countries on the other side of Germany — Poland and Czechoslovakia. The wall also made the German people, who had been alarmed by the construction of the Maginot line, feel more secure.

The West Wall was much looser in design than the Maginot line and included no huge underground forts like the French *ouvrages.* Along the border itself were a series of mines, barbed-wire entanglements, foxholes, trenches, and observation posts. Fifteen hundred or so feet behind these barriers came the heavily fortified Army Zone.

The Army Zone was largely composed of concrete *pillboxes,* so named because they had the curved, circular shape of a container for pills. The pillboxes were arranged in cluster patterns so they could cover one another with antitank and machine gun fire in case of an enemy attack. Each pillbox was set low in the ground for protection and was designed to be manned by ten or fifteen soldiers. Like the *avant-postes* in the Maginot line, the pillboxes contained not only gun chambers but also storage rooms for food and ammunition and living quarters for the soldiers.

Barbed-wire formations encircled the pillboxes, and in front of them ran lines of concrete antitank obstacles called "dragon's teeth." These were triangular in shape, and set in rows of four or five with the highest "teeth" in back. They stretched through towns and forests, over hills and marshes, and sometimes even bridged small rivers.

Unlike the Maginot line, the bulk of the German forces were not stationed in the pillboxes of the West Wall. Only a skeleton force garrisoned

OPPOSITE, TOP: *Antitank traps on the West Wall* (National Archives)
BOTTOM: *A concrete pillbox on the West Wall* (National Archives)

the wall, while most of the troops remained in barracks at the back of the Army Zone, where they could respond quickly to an alarm from either the Army Zone or the Air Defense Zone to the rear.

The Germans, in contrast to the French, believed that aircraft would play a crucial role in the next war. Consequently, the Air Defense Zone contained searchlights, antiaircraft guns, and military airports for fighter planes.

Over five hundred thousand German army engineers and personnel, and civilian workers, rushed to complete the West Wall as soon as possible. By mid-1939 this labor force had poured over six million tons of concrete, laid three million rolls of barbed wire, and constructed twenty-two thousand individual pillboxes and shelters.

Meanwhile the French, reacting to the West Wall, extended the Maginot line by building a string of forts on France's eastern border, down along the Rhine. They also added some fortifications to the northern end of the line, near the border with Belgium. But they didn't extend the line all the way to the Atlantic coast for fear of offending their Belgian allies and making them feel excluded. That proved to be a fatal mistake.

In September 1939, Nazi Germany marched into Poland. Great Britain and France honored their alliance with Poland and declared war on Germany. World War II had begun.

Poland fell in a few weeks under the onslaught of German bombs and troops, but virtually nothing happened on the western front during the fall and winter of 1939–1940. French soldiers filled the forts of the Maginot line and German troops manned the pillboxes of the West Wall, but neither moved against the other. Journalists labeled this strange period the "phony war."

Down in the barracks of the Maginot line, water seeped through cracks in the concrete walls, and the men bumped their heads when they tried to climb into their cramped bunks. One French soldier on duty on the line described what it was like in a letter to his wife: "Before you, there's an unknown countryside, a black night. The nearest post is several hundred yards away. Your feet are frozen in their stiff boots. Your helmet weighs heavily. Your eyes are tired from looking without seeing."

The most dangerous aspect of the Maginot line, though, was the mood of complacency it bred. A British military observer, Lieutenant General Alanbrooke, wrote after visiting the line in February 1940: "A sense of false

OPPOSITE: *French soldiers trying to relax in a barracks on the*
Maginot line (Imperial War Museum)

security is engendered, a feeling of sitting behind an impregnable iron fence;
and should the fence perchance be broken, the French fighting spirit might
well be brought crumbling with it."

The "phony war" came to an abrupt end in April 1940, when Germany
invaded first Denmark and then Norway. At the same time Reich Marshal
Hermann Goering, commander of the German air force, declared that Germany was going to attack two points along the Maginot line and was
prepared to lose five hundred thousand men in the process, as well as 80
percent of its air force.

The French immediately reinforced the casemates and *ouvrages* of the
line, but Goering's speech proved to be a ruse. Instead the German army
invaded Holland and Belgium, and swept down into France through the
Ardennes Forest along one of the same routes they had used in World
War I.

By early June, the German army had completely surrounded the Maginot line, cutting it off from the rest of France. The Germans managed to
capture one small, outlying fort. But the defenders of the rest fought bravely
on, despite the fact that they were besieged on all sides. Although the great
ouvrages suffered damage, none of them was ever actually overcome. Their
garrisons surrendered only after France declared an armistice with Germany
on June 17, 1940.

Adolf Hitler himself came to France to sign the armistice on June 22,
and afterward he toured several of the Maginot line *ouvrages* — those giant
forts that had cost so much and achieved so little.

The last of the great defensive walls of World War II was the Atlantic
Wall, which the Germans started building along the Atlantic seacoast after
the fall of France. Its purpose was to prevent any landing on the coast by
a British naval force, and the original plans called for it to extend all the
way from Holland to the Spanish border.

Because the coast to be defended was so long, responsibility for building fortifications along it was divided between the German army, navy, and
air force. The navy constructed artillery emplacements around harbors and
ports. The army erected pillboxes for machine and antitank guns along the
stretches of coast in between. The air force laid out airfields for fighter
planes. Hitler, who had studied art as a young man, took a personal interest
in the project and drew sketches for pillboxes and artillery casemates.

Construction of the Atlantic Wall was speeded up after the United
States entered the war on the side of England on December 8, 1941. The

original plans proved too ambitious, however, and only places of major strategic importance were fully guarded by artillery casemates and pillboxes. As Albert Speer, head of Germany's wartime production, said later: "In 1942 a complete line of concrete pillboxes spaced close enough to offer mutual protection would have far exceeded the capacity of the German construction industry."

After the Soviet Union defeated the German army at Stalingrad early in 1943, the threat of an Allied invasion in the west increased. Field Marshal Erwin Rommel was appointed German inspector of fortifications and toured the entire Atlantic coast from the North Sea to the Spanish frontier.

Rommel was appalled by what he found. Most of the guns the navy had installed around the major ports were in bombproof steel cupolas, but many of the army's seacoast batteries were only lightly dug in, with no overhead protection. In many places even such basic fortifications as anti-tank obstacles, mines, and barbed wire had been neglected.

After submitting his report to Hitler and Speer, Rommel, in January 1944, was named commander in chief of an area extending from the Netherlands to the Loire River in southern France. In the next few months he raced against time to build up the shore defenses before the Allied invasion, which was expected at any moment.

Rommel assembled a huge labor force of German army men and civilian workers, French conscripted laborers, and Polish and Russian prisoners of war. Working day and night, they managed to cover more than half of the artillery emplacements along the coast, built hundreds of new pillboxes, and connected as many of the installations as possible with underground communication tunnels.

Rommel put special emphasis on shore defenses. The work force erected rows of obstacles, mined and otherwise, to prevent boats from getting ashore. They laid barbed wire and more obstacles and mines along the beach itself and around all the newly built bunkers and pillboxes.

Construction activities became harder to sustain as supplies ran short and Allied bombing raids intensified. During three days in May 1944, only 47 of the 240 railroad cars of cement needed for the Normandy coast fortifications arrived at their destination. Soon afterward all supplies stopped.

Still, an amazing job had been done. On the more than a thousand miles of coast Rommel had taken command of in January 1944, ninety-three hundred fortifications had been completed by June 6, the day the Allies landed on the beaches of Normandy.

Despite the almost superhuman effort that went into its construction, the Atlantic Wall proved ineffective as a defensive barrier. The Allies created their own artificial harbors out at sea, and by using a wide variety of landing craft and armored vehicles, they were able to break through the fortifications

ABOVE: *Shore defenses along the Atlantic Wall, 1944* (The Library of Congress)
BELOW: *German soldier on duty in a pillbox on the Atlantic Wall* (The Library of Congress)

*U.S. tank passing through line of "dragons' teeth" on the West
Wall, April 1945* (Imperial War Museum)

of the wall quite quickly. The port city of Le Havre fell in forty-eight hours, the cities of Calais and Boulogne in six days.

Later Albert Speer commented on the German defeat: "In building the Atlantic Wall we consumed in barely two years of intensive construction 17,300,000 cubic yards of concrete. In addition, the armaments factories were deprived of 1,200,000 metric tons of steel. All this expenditure was sheer waste. The enemy bypassed these defenses within two weeks of the first landing. . . . Our whole plan of defense proved to be irrelevant."

The Germans didn't fare any better when Allied armies under General Dwight D. Eisenhower reached the West Wall fortifications nine months later, in March 1945.

Earlier in the war many of the West Wall's guns, tank traps, and barbed-wire entanglements had been removed for use on other fronts. By the spring of 1945, only the pillboxes and other permanent installations remained in many places, and some of these were being used as civilian air-raid shelters and agricultural warehouses.

A small force of engineers was still on duty in the West Wall fortifications. Together with retreating German troops, they put up a last-ditch stand against General Eisenhower's advancing army. But it was no use. On March 23, 1945, Eisenhower crossed the Rhine and the last organized resistance on the West Wall ceased.

The West Wall, like the Maginot line and the Atlantic Wall, had failed to do its job; it had failed to repel the enemy. To most observers, this seemed decisive proof that, under the conditions of twentieth-century warfare, defensive walls were useless.

If further proof were needed it came five months later in August 1945, when atomic bombs were dropped on Hiroshima and Nagasaki, Japan. In the face of their destructiveness, it was impossible to imagine how any defense could be effective.

A WALL IN SPACE?

A view of the Berlin Wall (German Information Center)

Even though no one believed that any sort of concrete wall could protect a city or a country from the atomic bomb, some defensive walls were still built for other purposes after World War II. Probably the most famous of these was the Berlin Wall.

After Nazi Germany surrendered in 1945, the four victorious Allies — Great Britain, France, the Soviet Union, and the United States — divided its capital city, Berlin, into four occupation zones. Each zone was administered by one of the Allies. Eventually the three western zones merged into the half of the city called West Berlin, while the Soviet zone became known as East Berlin.

The entire city was an island in the midst of the Soviet zone of Germany, the large part of the country that the Soviet army had occupied in the last months of the war. This zone later became a separate country, the German Democratic Republic, or East Germany. It was allied with the Soviet Union just as the Federal Republic of Germany, or West Germany, was allied to the western powers.

Attracted by the political freedom and economic prosperity of the west, more than three million people left East Germany between 1945 and 1961. It was a relatively simple matter then to take a subway train to West Berlin, and fly from there to West Germany.

As the exodus continued, the East German authorities grew increasingly alarmed. For among those leaving were many doctors, scientists, engineers, and other professionals whom the country badly needed. East Germany decided that something drastic would have to be done to stop the migration. The result was the Berlin Wall.

Literally overnight on August 13, 1961, East German soldiers and workers cut off public transportation between East and West Berlin, blocked all streets connecting the two, and flung up hasty barriers of barbed wire along the twenty-eight-mile border between the two halves of the city.

The western allies denounced this action but did not attempt to remove the barriers. They feared that a clash along the border between the two Berlins might lead to a larger conflict, and perhaps even trigger World War III.

In the weeks and months that followed, the East Germans finished the job they had started. They demolished many houses and buildings near the wall and bricked up the windows and doors of others so that they could not be used in escape attempts. Then they cleared a three-hundred-foot stretch of land on their side of the wall and planted it with mines, barbed-wire entanglements, antivehicle traps, and runs for fierce police dogs.

The wall itself was built of concrete blocks raised to a height of twelve feet and topped with barbed wire. Visitors and tourists wanting to go from

OPPOSITE AND OVERLEAF: *Views of the Berlin Wall* (German Information Center)

West to East had to pass through one of several fortified checkpoints, where their papers were examined by East German border guards.

In time the East Germans extended the wall around the entire hundred-mile circumference of West Berlin by erecting an electrified chain-link fence. As many as fifteen thousand East German soldiers stood guard in watchtowers along the wall and fence, and patrolled the cleared border area with orders to shoot unauthorized persons on sight.

Despite these obstacles, thousands of East Germans since 1961 have tried to get across the wall by climbing over it, tunneling under it, or crashing through it. Many have succeeded, but at least seventy-five others have died in the attempt.

To ease some of the tensions created by the Wall, the United States, Great Britain, and France joined the Soviet Union in signing a new Berlin agreement in 1970. It encouraged the two German states to work out arrangements between themselves for easier access between the two halves of Berlin. As a result, West Berliners since 1972 have been able to cross over into East Germany to see their relatives or do business, and East Germans of retirement age have been permitted to move to the West.

The wall still stands, however, and will no doubt continue to stand as long as Germany remains divided into two separate countries. Today thousands of tourists each year climb up to platforms on the wall's western side and look out over the empty, frightening stretch of no-man's-land that lies between the wall and East Berlin.

Seeing the wall at first hand, many tourists are reminded of city walls of the past. Unlike them, however, the Berlin Wall is equipped with barbed wire and machine guns. And its main purpose is not to keep an enemy from entering the city, but to prevent its own inhabitants from leaving.

In many countries, east and west, the builders of postwar fortifications borrowed ideas from the defensive walls of World War II. They housed intercontinental ballistic missiles in underground concrete silos that were similar to the artillery casemates of the Maginot line. They also dug deep shelters, like the command centers of the line's *ouvrages,* to protect their main government offices from a nuclear attack.

Of course no one knows how well such defenses would function in case of an all-out atomic war. As one British military publication has commented, "The best defense against the atomic bomb is not to be there when it goes off."

Recently some U.S. military experts have proposed that an entirely new kind of defensive wall be developed. It would be located in space and would be composed of fifty or sixty unmanned satellites, each armed with a short-range laser beam. If the Soviet Union or any other enemy launched a wave of nuclear ballistic missiles, the laser beams would be aimed at them. So many beams would go into action all at once, the experts say, that the enemy missiles would be attacked and destroyed before they could reach their targets.

Other scientists argue that a space wall of satellites would never work. For one thing, they say, it couldn't intercept low-flying or shorter-range weapons. For another, it would be quite easy to ruin the system's effectiveness. An enemy could try to shoot down the satellites before launching their missiles. Or they might jam the system's communications, or confuse its aiming mechanisms by sending up a large number of decoy missiles.

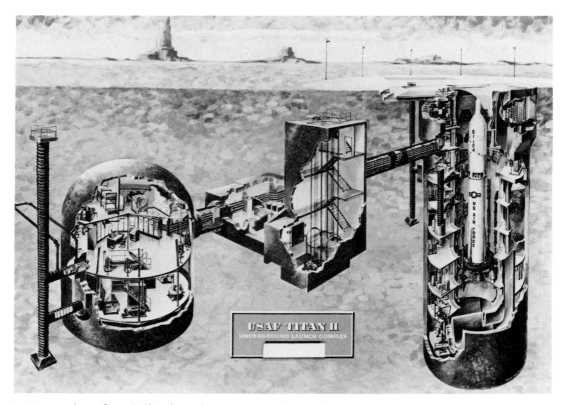

Cutaway view of a missile silo and underground support installations (U.S. Air Force)

OPPOSITE: *Minuteman III missile in an underground silo* (U.S. Air Force)

Even if these problems were somehow overcome, it's highly unlikely that such a defense system would ever be perfect. And it would have to be perfect to protect a nation's cities and factories from nuclear destruction. In 1983 the Soviet Union had more than nine thousand strategic nuclear weapons. If only 5 percent of them, or 450 missiles, reached their targets in the United States, it would be more than enough to wipe out all major centers of activity in the country.

Ever since prehistoric times, as we have seen, people have built defensive walls. Whether they were made of mammoth bones, or mud bricks, or reinforced concrete, their purpose was the same: to protect the people of a tribe, a city, a castle, or an entire country from attack by an enemy.

None of the walls was ever entirely successful. If an enemy was determined enough, he usually found some way to get over, around, under, or through the wall. In spite of this, nations and states continued to build defensive walls. Their size alone seemed to give people a sense of security, even if the wall later proved to be almost totally ineffective, like the huge forts of the Maginot line.

Today, in the atomic age, some leaders and scientists are still seeking the ultimate defensive wall. But perhaps the time has finally come to admit that no such wall is possible. Confronted by nuclear weapons, any nation that wants to feel secure in the future will have to reach some sort of understanding with its enemies. It can't hope to achieve security by building a wall.

GLOSSARY

Bailey — The fenced-in area that stood in front of the motte, or mound, in a motte-and-bailey castle.

Ballistic missile — A projectile that ascends into the air on its own internally guided power, and then falls freely on a predetermined line to its target.

Barbican — A large guard tower built beside a gate or bridge leading into a city or castle.

Bastion — A projecting part of a fortification, usually triangular in shape and consisting of an embankment of earth faced with brick or stone.

Battering ram — An ancient military machine composed of a heavy wooden beam mounted on a wheeled wooden framework. In siege warfare, the ram was used to batter down the gates and walls of enemy fortifications.

Battlement — A low wall built on top of a castle wall, tower, or fort. A battlement had low spaces in it through which defending soldiers could fire a gun or drop a rock on the enemy below.

Bombard — An early type of cannon that hurled stones or other heavy objects.

Bunker — A fortified position, usually built partly or entirely underground and designed to protect a gun emplacement or a squad of soldiers.

Casemate — A shellproof or armored enclosure with openings for guns, as in the wall of a fortress.

Castle — A fortified dwelling house.

Concentric castle — A castle with two or more defensive walls around it.

Cordon — A projecting band of stone on the surface of a wall. It made climbing the wall more difficult.

Counterscarp — The outer slope or wall of a ditch or moat in a fortification.

Cupola — A dome-shaped, armor-plated, revolving gun turret in a fortress.

Donjon — The heavily fortified inner tower or keep of a castle.

Dugout — A large hole dug in the ground and often covered or reinforced with logs or concrete. Used as a bomb shelter and in trench warfare.

Embrasure — An opening in a battlement or parapet through which arrows and guns could be fired.

Escarp — Ground formed into a steep slope or bank as part of a fortification. Also the name given to the near side of a ditch or moat.

Fortification — A defensive earthwork or wall used to help protect a town, castle, or military position.

Garderobe — A toilet built into the wall of a castle.

Glacis — An embankment of earth sloping gradually up to a fortification so that attackers will be exposed to defending arrows or gunfire.

Hoard — A temporary wooden walkway built about five or six feet out from the top of a parapet. Holes in the floor of the hoard allowed the defenders to shoot arrows, hurl rocks, or drop boiling oil on attackers below.

Keep — The walled central area of a castle. A keep usually contained living quarters for the nobleman, his family, and their servants; storerooms for food and valuables; and a chapel.

Machicolation — An opening in the floor of a stone gallery built out from the top of a city or castle wall, or a hole in the floor above a gate or other entrance. Rocks and boiling liquids could be dropped down through a machicolation onto the heads of unwanted visitors below.

Mangonel — An ancient military apparatus for hurling heavy stones and other missiles at an enemy fortress.

Merlon — The solid part of a battlement or parapet, between two openings, or embrasures.

Motte — A hill or mound.

Ouvrage — The French word for the huge underground forts in the Maginot line.

Palisade — A row of large, pointed stakes set in the ground to form a fence used for fortification or defense.

Parade — The central, ground-level area of a fort where troops regularly gathered for an assembly or review.

Parapet — A low wall used to screen troops from frontal enemy fire, often constructed along the top or sides of a defensive wall.

Pillbox — An enclosed gun emplacement made of concrete and steel.

Portcullis — A wooden or metal grille, often with metal spikes across the bottom. It could be dropped down over the entrance to a castle, thus blocking the way.

Postern — A hidden entrance or exit in the wall of an ancient city or castle.

Rampart — A wall of earth or stone, frequently topped by a parapet. The rampart encircled a city, castle, or fort, defending them from attackers.

Ravelin — A triangular defensive work, usually located in the ditch in front of a fortress.

Redan — A triangular fortification consisting of two walls pointed toward the enemy and an opening at the back.

Sap — An extended, narrow trench for approaching or undermining an enemy position.

Sapper — A soldier employed in digging saps, or forward trenches.

Satellite — A man-made object designed to orbit a celestial body like the earth, the moon, or another planet.

Siege tower — A wheeled wooden structure, two or more stories high. Archers standing on the upper levels could fire directly at the defenders atop a city or castle wall.

Silo — An underground shelter for a missile.

Tenaille trace — An additional defensive wall of masonry erected in front of the bastioned wall in a fortress.

Terreplein — A level platform behind a rampart. Guns are usually mounted on the terreplein.

Trench — A long, narrow ditch from which the earth is thrown up in front as a parapet. Used in battle for cover and concealment.

BIBLIOGRAPHY

Bergstrom, Theo. *Hadrian's Wall.* London: Bergstrom & Boyle Books, 1975

Bruce, J. Collingwood. *The Handbook to the Roman Wall.* London: Longmans, Green & Co., 1921

Burke, John. *The Castle in Medieval England.* London: B. T. Batsford, Ltd., 1978

Catton, Bruce. *The Coming Fury.* New York: Doubleday, 1961

———. *Never Call Retreat.* New York: Doubleday, 1965

Cottrell, Leonard. *The Tiger of Ch'in.* New York: Holt, Rinehart, and Winston, 1962

De La Croix, Horst. *Military Considerations in City Planning.* New York: George Braziller, 1972

Dulles, Eleanor Lansing. *Berlin: The Wall Is Not Forever.* Chapel Hill: University of North Carolina Press, 1967

Dupuy, Ernest and Trevor N. *The Encyclopedia of Military History from 3500 B.C. to the Present.* New York: Harper & Row, 1977

Fry, Plantagenet Somerset. *British Medieval Castles.* New York: A. S. Barnes, 1975

Fujioka, Michio. *Japanese Castles.* Osaka: Hoikusha Publishing Co., 1968

Hirai, Kiyoshi. *Feudal Architecture of Japan.* New York: Weatherhill, 1973

Hogg, Ian V. *Fortress: A History of Military Defense.* New York: St. Martin's Press, 1977

Horne, Alistair. *To Lose a Battle: France 1940.* Boston: Little, Brown and Co., 1969

Hughes, Quentin. *Military Architecture.* New York: St. Martin's Press, 1974

Klein, Richard G. *Ice-Age Hunters of the Ukraine.* Chicago: University of Chicago Press, 1973

Kotker, Norman, ed. *The Horizon History of China.* New York: American Heritage Publishing Co., Inc., 1969

Macaulay, David. *Castle.* Boston: Houghton Mifflin Co., 1977

Mallory, Keith, and Arvid Ottar. *The Architecture of War.* New York: Pantheon Books, 1973

Pachter, Henry M. *Modern Germany.* Boulder, Colorado: Westview Press, 1978

Peterson, Harold L. *Forts in America.* New York: Charles Scribner's Sons, 1964

Poole, Austin Lane, ed. *Medieval England, Volume 1.* Oxford: Oxford University Press, 1958

Speer, Albert. *Inside the Third Reich.* New York: Macmillan Co., 1970

Toy, Sidney. *A History of Fortification: From 3000 B.C. to A.D. 1700.* London: William Heinemann Ltd., 1955

Viollet le Duc, Eugène. *An Essay on the Military Architecture of the Middle Ages.* Westport, CT: Greenwood Press, 1976

Whitehouse, Ruth. *The First Cities.* New York: E. P. Dutton, 1977

INDEX